HTML
Pocket Reference

Jennifer Niederst

Beijing • Cambridge • Farnham • Köln • Paris • Sebastopol • Taipei • Tokyo

HTML Pocket Reference

by Jennifer Niederst

Copyright © 2000 O'Reilly & Associates, Inc. All rights reserved. Printed in the United States of America. Published by O'Reilly & Associates, Inc., 101 Morris Street, Sebastopol, CA 95472.

Editor: Richard Koman

Production Editor: Colleen Gorman

Cover Design: Hanna Dyer

Printing History:

January 2000:　　　First Edition

[9/00]

1-56592-579-3
[C]

Table of Contents

HTML Pocket Reference

Introduction

This pocket reference provides a concise, yet thorough, listing of HTML tags and attributes specified by the W3C HTML 4.0 Specification, Netscape Navigator, and Internet Explorer.

Using This Book

The majority of this reference is an alphabetical listing of tags and their attributes with explanations and browser support information.

Following the alphabetical tag list are two sections that provide more context for using HTML. "Tag Groups" lists tags that are related in functionality, and "Tag Structures" provides examples of how standard web page elements are constructed.

So, for example, if you are making a table, the "Table Tags" section lists all the tags that pertain to tables, and the "Basic Table" examples show the basic structure of how the table tags work together.

The book also provides several useful charts, including Character Entities, Decimal to Hexadecimal Conversions, and Color Names.

For Further Reading

More in-depth explanations of HTML and web design can be found in O'Reilly and Associates' *Web Design in a Nutshell* by Jennifer Niederst and *HTML: The Definitive Guide* by Chuck Musciano and Bill Kennedy. Also useful is *Webmaster in a Nutshell* by Stephen Spainhour and Robert Eckstein.

The browser support information in this book was provided by the HTML Compendium created by Ron Woodall. I encourage you to check out the Compendium's site (*http://www.htmlcompendium.org*) for extremely in-depth explanations of HTML tags, attributes, and values and the browsers that support them.

Conventions Used in This Book

The correct syntax appears to the right of each tag and indicates whether the tag is a container (with an end tag) or stands alone. Browser support information is indicated below each tag. Browsers that do not support the tag are shown in gray. A superscript D indicates that the tag has been deprecated by the specification or browser. Attribute support is indicated in italics in the attribute description.

Alphabetical Tag List

<a>   <a>...</a>

NN: 2, 3, 4 · MSIE: 2, 3, 4, 5 · HTML 4 · WebTV · Opera3

Defines an *anchor* within the document. An anchor is used to link to another document. It can also serve to label a fragment of a document (also called a *named anchor*), which is used as a reference for linking to a specific point in an HTML document.

Attributes

`href=`*`url`*

> Specifies the URL of the target destination.

`method=`*`value`*

> Specifies a list of names, each representing a particular document-processing method, usually an application name. It is browser-dependent and is rarely used in practice.

`name=`*`text`*

> Identifies and names a portion of the document (called a "fragment"). The fragment can be referenced within a URL, preceded by the hash (#) symbol. See the following "Link Examples."

`rel=next|prev|head|toc|parent|child|index|glossary`

> *Not supported by Navigator or Opera.* Establishes a relationship between the current document and the target document.

`rev=`*`relationship`*

> *Not supported by Navigator or Opera.* Specifies the relationship from the target back to the source (the opposite of the `rel` attribute). The relationship options are the same as for the `rel` attribute.

`title=`*`text`*

> Specifies a title for the target document.

`target=`*`name`*`|_blank|_self|_parent|_top`

> *Not supported by WebTV or Internet Explorer 2.0 and earlier.* Specifies the name of the window or frame in which the target document should be displayed. The standard target names work as follows:

> `_blank`

>> Opens a new, unnamed browser window.

_self

> Loads the linked document into the same frame or window as the source document. This is the default target for all links.

_parent

> Linked document loads into the parent frame (one step up in the frame hierarchy).

_top

> Causes document to load at the top-level window containing the link, replacing any frames currently displayed.

urn=*urn*

> Specifies a Universal Resource Name (URN) for the referenced document. URN syntax is currently not defined so this attribute has no practical use.

New in HTML 4.0 Specification

accesskey=*character*

> Assigns an access key (shortcut key command) to the link. Access keys are also used for form fields. The value is a single character.

charset=*charset*

> Specifies the character encoding (e.g., iso-8859-1) of the target document.

coords=*x,y coordinates*

> *HTML 4.0 only.* Specifies the x,y coordinates for a clickable area in an imagemap. HTML 4.0 proposes that client-side imagemaps could be replaced with an <object> tag containing the image and a set of anchor tags defining the "hot" areas (with shapes and coordinate attributes). This system has not yet been implemented by browsers.

`hreflang=`*language code*

Specifies the base language of the target document. For a listing of the 2-character language codes see *http://babel.alis.com/langues/iso639.htm.*

`shape=default`
> `circle x,y,r`
> `rect x,y,w,h`
> `poly x1,y1,x2,y2...`
> `polygon x1,y1,x2,y2...`

HTML 4.0 only. Specifies the shape and coordinates of a clickable area in an imagemap. This is only used in the `<a>` tag as part of HTML 4.0's proposal to replace client-side imagemaps with a combination of `<object>` and `<a>` tags. This system has not yet been implemented by browsers.

`tabindex=`*number*

Specifies the position of the current element in the tabbing order for the current document. The value must be between 0 and 32767. Including this attribute allows users to tab through the links on a page.

`type=`*MIME type*

Specifies the content type (MIME type) of the defined content.

Link examples

To a local file:

```
<A HREF="filename.html">...</A>
```

To an external file:

```
<A HREF="http://server/path/file.html">...</A>
```

To a named anchor:

```
<A HREF="http://server/path/
file.html#fragment">...</A>
```

To a named anchor in the same file:

```
<A HREF="#fragment">...</A>
```

<a>

To send an email message:

```
<A HREF="mailto:username@domain">...</A>
```

To a file on an FTP server:

```
<A HREF="ftp://server/path/filename">...</A>
```

<abbr>   `<abbr>...</abbr>`

NN: 2, 3, 4 · MSIE: 2, 3, 4, 5 · **HTML 4** · WebTV · Opera3

Identifies the enclosed text as an abbreviation. It has no inherent effect on text display, but can be used as an element selector in a style sheet.

Attributes

`title=text`

Provides the full expression for the abbreviation. This may be useful for non-visual browsers and search engines.

Example

```
<ABBR TITLE="Massachusetts">Mass.</ABBR>
```

<acronym>   `<acronym>...</acronym>`

NN: 2, 3, 4 · MSIE: 2, 3, 4, 5 · **HTML 4** · WebTV · Opera3

Indicates an acronym. It has no inherent effect on text display, but can be used as an element selector in a style sheet.

Attributes

`title=text`

Provides the full expression for the acronym. This may be useful for non-visual browsers and search engines.

Example

```
<ACRONYM TITLE="World Wide Web">WWW</ACRONYM>
```

<address>   <address>...</address>

NN: 2, 3, 4 · MSIE: 2, 3, 4, 5 · HTML 4 · WebTV · Opera3

Identifies ownership or authorship information, typically at the beginning or end of a document. Addresses are generally formatted in italic type with a line break (but no extra space) above and below.

<applet>   <applet>...</applet>

NN: 2, 3, 4 · MSIE: 2, 3, 4, 5 · HTML 4ᴰ · WebTV · Opera3

This tag, introduced by Navigator 2.0, is used to place a Java applet on the web page. It is deprecated in the HTML 4.0 Specification in favor of <object>.

Attributes

align=center|left|right
: Aligns the applet and allows text to wrap around it (same as image alignment).

alt=*text*
: Provides alternate text if the applet cannot be displayed.

code=*class*
: Specifies the class name of the code to be executed (required).

codebase=*url*
: URL from which the code is retrieved.

height=*number*
: Height of the applet window in pixels.

hspace=*number*
: Holds a specified number of pixels space clear to the left and right of the applet window.

name=*text*
: Names the applet for reference elsewhere on the page.

`vspace=`*`number`*

Holds a specified number of pixels space clear above and below the applet window.

`width=`*`number`*

Width of the applet window in pixels.

<area>

NN: 2, 3, 4 · MSIE: 2, 3, 4, 5 · HTML 4 · WebTV · Opera3

The area tag is used within the `<map>` tag of a client-side imagemap to define a specific "hot" (clickable) area.

Attributes

`coords=`*`values`*

Specifies a list of comma-separated pixel coordinates that define a "hot" area of an imagemap. The specific syntax for the coordinates varies by shape as follows:

Rectangles

If `shape=rect` or `rectangle`, use the coordinates `x1,y1,x2,y2`, where `x1,y1` are the coordinates for the point at the top, left corner and `x2,y2` are the coordinates for the bottom, right corner.

Circles

If `shape=circ` or `circle`, use the coordinates `x,y,r`, where `x` and `y` are the coordinates of the center-point, and `r` is the length of the radius.

Polygons

If `shape=poly`, use the coordinates `x1,y1,x2,y2, x3,y3,...`, where the values are sets of `x,y` coordinates for points around the path that surrounds the area.

`href=`*`url`*

Specifies the URL for a specific area.

---

nohref
> Defines a "mouse-sensitive" area in an imagemap for which there is no action when the user clicks in the area.

shape=rect|rectangle|circ|circle|poly|
polygon
> Defines the shape of the clickable area. The shape name must be accompanied by the appropriate set of coordinates (see syntax under coords attribute above).

\<b> <div style="float:right">\<b>...</b></div>

NN: 2, 3, 4 · MSIE: 2, 3, 4, 5 · HTML 4 · WebTV · Opera3

Enclosed text is rendered in bold.

\<basefont> <div style="float:right">\<basefont></div>

NN: 2, 3, 4 · MSIE: 2, 3, 4, 5 · HTML 4[D] · WebTV · Opera3

Specifies certain font attributes for text following the tag. It can be used within the \<head> tags to apply to the entire document, or within the body of the document to apply to the subsequent text. This tag is not part of the HTML standard; Cascading Style Sheets are the preferred method to achieve the functionality of \<basefont>.

Attributes

color=#rrggbb or *name*
> *Internet Explorer 3.0+ only*. Sets the color of the following text using hexadecimal RGB values.

face=*font*
> *Internet Explorer 3.0+ only*. Sets the font for the following text.

size=1|2|3|4|5|6|7|+1|+2|+3|+4|-1|-2
> Sets the basefont size using the HTML size values from 1 to 7 (or relative values based on the default value of 3).

Subsequent relative size settings will be based on this value.

<base> <base>

NN: 2, 3, 4 · MSIE: 2, 3, 4, 5 · HTML 4 · WebTV · Opera3

Specifies the base URL for all relative URLs in the document. Place this within the <head> of the document.

Attributes

href=*url*

Specifies the URL to be used.

target=*name*

Defines the default target window for all links in the document. Often used to target frames. This attribute is not supported in Internet Explorer 2.0.

<bdo> <bdo>...</bdo>

NN: 2, 3, 4 · MSIE: 2, 3, 4, 5 · HTML 4 · WebTV · Opera3

Stands for "bi-directional override" and specifies that the enclosed text flows in the opposite direction from the surrounding text. It is part of the W3C's efforts toward internationalization. One use might be to identify a span of Arabic text (which reads right to left) in English text.

<bgsound> <bgsound>

NN: 2, 3, 4 · MSIE: 2, 3, 4, 5 · HTML 4 · WebTV · Opera3

Plays an audio file automatically in the background when the document loads in the browser.

<blockquote>

Attributes

`src=url`

> This required attribute provides the URL of the audio file to be downloaded and played.

`loop=number|infinite`

> Sets the number of times the sound file should play. The value can be a number or set to infinite.

<big>

`<big>...</big>`

NN: 2, 3, 4 · MSIE: 2, 3, 4, 5 · HTML 4 · WebTV · Opera3

Sets the type one font size larger than the surrounding text. It is equivalent to `<font size="+1">`.

<blink>

`<blink>...</blink>`

NN: 2, 3, 4 · MSIE: 2, 3, 4, 5 · HTML 4 · WebTV · Opera3

Causes the contained text to flash on and off.

<blockquote>

`<blockquote>...</blockquote>`

NN: 2, 3, 4 · MSIE: 2, 3, 4, 5 · HTML 4 · WebTV · Opera3

Identifies enclosed text as quoted material. Blockquotes are generally displayed with an indent on the left and right margins and added space above and below the paragraph.

Note that:

- Some older browsers display blockquote material in italic, making it difficult to read.

- Browsers are inconsistent in the way they display images within blockquotes. Some align the graphic with the indented blockquote margin; others align the image with the normal margin of paragraph text. It is a good idea to test on a variety of browsers.

<body>

<body>...</body>

NN: 2, 3, 4 · MSIE: 2, 3, 4, 5 · HTML 4 · WebTV · Opera3

Defines the beginning and the end of the document body. The body contains the content of the document (the part that is displayed in the browser window). Attributes to the <body> tag affect the entire document.

Attributes

alink=*#rrggbb* or *color name*

> Sets the color of active links (i.e., the color while the mouse button is held down during a "click"). Color is specified in hexadecimal RGB values or by standard web color name.

background=*url*

> Provides the URL to a graphic file to be used as a tiling graphic in the background of the document.

bgcolor=*#rrggbb* or *color name*

> Sets the color of the background for the document.

link=*#rrggbb* or *color name*

> Sets the default color for all the links in the document.

text=*#rrggbb* or *color name*

> Sets the default color for all the text in the document.

vlink=*#rrggbb* or *color name*

> Sets the color of the visited links for the document.

Navigator 4.0 only

marginwidth=*number*

> Specifies the distance (in pixels) between the left browser edge and the beginning of the text and graphics in the window.

`marginheight=`*number*

> Specifies the distance (in pixels) between the top edge of the browser and the top edge of text or graphics in the window.

Internet Explorer only
`bgproperties=fixed`

> When set to "fixed," the background image does not scroll with the document content.

`leftmargin=`*number*

> Specifies the distance (in pixels) between the left browser edge and the beginning of the text and graphics in the window.

`topmargin=`*number*

> Specifies the distance (in pixels) between the top edge of the browser and the top edge of text or graphics in the window.

Setting margins

Because Navigator and Internet Explorer support different margin attributes, you may need to specify the margin attribute twice within the \<body> tag to ensure full browser compatibility, as follows:

```
<BODY MARGINWIDTH=0 LEFTMARGIN=0>
```

\

\

NN: 2, 3, 4 · MSIE: 2, 3, 4, 5 · HTML 4 · WebTV · Opera3

Breaks the text and begins a new line, but does not add extra space as the \<p> tag does.

Attributes
`clear=all|left|right`

> Breaks the text flow and resumes the next line after the specified margin is clear. This is often used to start the text below an aligned image (preventing text wrap).

<button>   <button> ... </button>

NN: 2, 3, **4** · **MSIE:** 2, 3, **4, 5** · **HTML 4** · WebTV · Opera3

Within a form, defines a "button" that functions similar to buttons created with the <input> tag, but allows for richer rendering possibilities. Buttons can contain content such as text and images.

Attributes

name=*text*

Assigns the control name for the element.

value=*text*

Assigns the initial value to the button.

type=submit|reset|button

Identifies the type of button: submit button (default value), a reset button, or a custom button (used with JavaScript), respectively.

<caption>   <caption>...</caption>

NN: 2, 3, **4** · **MSIE:** 2, 3, **4, 5** · **HTML 4** · WebTV · Opera3

Provides a brief summary of the table's contents or purpose. According to the W3C HTML 4.0 Specification, if used, the caption must immediately follow the <table> tag and precede all other tags. The width of the caption is determined by the width of the table. The caption's position as displayed in the browser can be controlled with the align attribute (or valign in Internet Explorer).

Attributes

align=top|bottom|left|right|center

Positions the caption relative to the table. This attribute has been deprecated by the W3C HTML 4.0 Specification in favor of style sheet positioning.

`summary=text`
> *W3C HTML 4.0 Specification only.* Used to provide a longer description of the table's contents for use by a speech- or Braille-based web browser.

`valign=top|bottom`
> *Internet Explorer 3.0 and higher only.* Positions the caption above or below the table (top is the default).

<center> <center>...</center>

NN: 2, 3, 4 · MSIE: 2, 3, 4, 5 · HTML 4^D · WebTV · Opera3

Centers the enclosed text horizontally on the page (same as `<DIV align=center>`). This tag is deprecated in the HTML 4.0 Specification in favor of style sheet controls for horizontal text alignment.

<cite> <cite>...</cite>

NN: 2, 3, 4 · MSIE: 2, 3, 4, 5 · HTML 4 · WebTV · Opera3

Denotes a citation—a reference to another document, especially books, magazines, articles, etc. Browsers generally display citations in italic.

<code> <code>...</code>

NN: 2, 3, 4 · MSIE: 2, 3, 4, 5 · HTML 4 · WebTV · Opera3

Denotes a code sample. Code is rendered in the browser's specified monospace font (usually Courier).

<col> <col>

NN: 2, 3, 4 · MSIE: 2, 3, 4, 5 · HTML 4 · WebTV · Opera3

Used within the `<table>` tag, this tag specifies properties for a column (or columns) within a column group (`<colgroup>`). Also, columns can share attributes (such as text

---

alignment) even if they are not part of a formal structural grouping.

Column groups and columns were introduced by Internet Explorer 3.0 and are now proposed by the HTML 4.0 Specification as a standard way to label table structure. They may also be useful in speeding the table display (i.e., the columns can be displayed incrementally without waiting for the entire contents of the table).

Attributes

align=left|right|center|char
> Specifies alignment of text in the cells of a column.

char=*character*
> Specifies a character along which the cell contents will be aligned. The default character is a decimal point (language-appropriate).

charoff=*length*
> Specifies the distance to the first alignment character (char) on each line. If a line doesn't use an alignment character, it should be horizontally shifted to end at the alignment position.

span=*number*
> Specifies the number of columns "spanned" by the <col> element (which shares its attributes with all the columns it spans).

valign=top|middle|bottom|baseline
> Specifies the vertical alignment of text in the cells of a column.

width=*pixels, percentage, n**
> Specifies the width (in pixels, percentage, or relative) of each column spanned by the <col> element. It overrides the width attribute of the containing <colgroup> element.

<colgroup>   <colgroup>...</colgroup>

NN: 2, 3, 4 · MSIE: 2, 3, 4, 5 · HTML 4 · WebTV · Opera3

Used within the <table> tag, this tag creates a column
group, a structural division within a table that can be
appointed attributes with style sheets or HTML. A table may
include more than one column group. The number of columns in a group is specified either by the value of the span
attribute or by a tally of columns <col> within the group.
Its end tag is optional.

Column groups and columns were introduced by Internet
Explorer 3.0 and are now proposed by the HTML 4.0 Specification as a standard way to label table structure. They
may also be useful in speeding the table display (i.e., the
columns can be displayed incrementally without waiting for
the entire contents of the table).

Attributes

align=left|right|center|char
: Specifies the alignment of text in the cells of a column
group.

char=*character*
: Specifies a character along which the cell contents will
be aligned. The default character is a decimal point (language-appropriate).

charoff=*length*
: Specifies the distance to the first alignment character
(char) on each line. If a line doesn't use an alignment
character, it should be horizontally shifted to end at the
alignment position.

span=*number*
: Specifies the number of columns in a column group. If
span is not specified, the default is 1.

`valign=top|middle|bottom|baseline`

Specifies the vertical alignment of text in the cells of a column group.

`width=pixels, percentage, n*`

Specifies a default width for each column in the current column group. Width can be measured in pixels, percentages, or defined as a relative size (*). For example, `2*` sets the column two times wider than the other columns; `0*` sets the column width at the minimum necessary to hold the column's contents.

`<dd>` `<dd>...</dd>`

NN: 2, 3, 4 · MSIE: 2, 3, 4, 5 · HTML 4 · WebTV · Opera3

Used within a Definition List (`<dl>`), this tag denotes the definition portion of an item within a definition list. The definition is usually displayed with an indented left margin. The closing tag is commonly omitted, but should be included when applying style sheets.

`<del>` `<del>...</del>`

NN: 2, 3, 4 · MSIE: 2, 3, 4, 5 · HTML 4 · WebTV · Opera3

Indicates deleted text. It has no inherent style qualities on its own, but may be used to hide deleted text from view or display it as strike-through text via style sheet controls. It may be useful for legal documents and any instance where edits need to be tracked. Its counterpart is inserted text (`<ins>`). Both can be used to indicate either inline or block-level elements.

<dl>

<dir>

<dir>...</dir>

NN: 2D, 3D, 4 · MSIE: 2, 3, 4, 5 · HTML 4D · WebTV · Opera3

Creates a directory list consisting of list items <li>. Directory lists were originally designed to display lists of files with short names, but they have been deprecated with the recommendation that unordered lists (<ul>) be used instead. Most browsers render directory lists the same as unordered lists (with bullets), although some will use a multicolumn format.

<div>

<div>...</div>

NN: 2, 3, 4 · MSIE: 2, 3, 4, 5 · HTML 4 · WebTV · Opera3

Denotes the beginning and end of a division of the page. First introduced in HTML 3.2 as a way to define a unique style for each division, only the alignment function (using the align attribute) was implemented by the major browsers.

The <div> tag has proven itself enormously valuable, however, when used in conjunction with style sheets.

Attributes

align=center|left|right

Aligns the text within the tags to the left, right, or center of the page.

<dl>

<dl>...</dl>

NN: 2, 3, 4 · MSIE: 2, 3, 4, 5 · HTML 4 · WebTV · Opera3

Indicates a definition list, consisting of terms (<dt>) and definitions (<dd>).

Attributes

`compact`

> Makes the list as small as possible. Few browsers support this attribute.

`<dt>` `<dt>...</dt>`

NN: 2, 3, 4 · MSIE: 2, 3, 4, 5 · HTML 4 · WebTV · Opera3

Used within a definition list (`<dl>`), this tag denotes the term portion of an item within a definition list. The closing tag is normally omitted, but should be included when applying style sheets.

`<em>` `<em>...</em>`

NN: 2, 3, 4 · MSIE: 2, 3, 4, 5 · HTML 4 · WebTV · Opera3

Indicates emphasized text. Nearly all browsers render emphasized text in italic.

`<embed>` `<embed>...</embed>`

NN: 2, 3, 4 · MSIE: 2, 3, 4, 5 · HTML 4 · WebTV · Opera3

Embeds an object into the web page. Embedded objects are most often multimedia files that require special plug-ins to display. Specific media types and their respective plug-ins may have additional proprietary attributes for controlling the playback of the file. The closing tag is not always required, but is recommended. The `<embed>` tag was dropped by the HTML 4.0 Specification in favor of `<object>` for adding multimedia elements to pages.

Attributes

`align=left|right|top|bottom`

> *Navigator 4.0 and Internet Explorer 4.0 only.* Controls the alignment of the media object relative to the surrounding

---

text. Top and bottom are vertical alignments. Left and right position the object on the left or right margin and allow text to wrap around it.

height=*number*

Specifies the height of the object in number of pixels. Some media types require this attribute.

hidden=yes|no

Hides the media file or player from view when set to yes.

hspace=*number*

Navigator 4.0 and Internet Explorer 4.0 only. Used in conjunction with the align attribute, this attribute specifies in number of pixels the amount of space to leave clear to the left and right of the media object.

name=*name*

Specifies a name for the embedded object. This is particularly useful for referencing the object from a script.

palette=foreground|background

Navigator 4.0 and Internet Explorer 4.0 only. This attributes applies to the Windows platform only. A value of foreground makes the palette used by the plug-in the foreground palette. Similarly, a value of background makes the plug-in use the background palette, which is also the default.

pluginspage=*url*

Navigator 4.0 and Internet Explorer 4.0 only. Specifies the URL for information on installing the appropriate plug-in.

src=*url*

Provides the URL to the file or object to be placed on the page. This is a required attribute.

units=pixels|en

Defines the measurement units used by height and width. The default is pixels. En units are half the point size of the body text.

---

vspace=*number*

> *Navigator 4.0 and Internet Explorer 4.0 only.* Used in conjunction with the align attribute, this attribute specifies (in pixels) the amount of space to leave clear above and below the media object.

width=*number*

> Specifies the width of the object in number of pixels. Some media types require this attribute.

Internet Explorer only

alt=*text*

> Provides alternative text when the media object cannot be displayed (same as for the <img> tag).

code=*filename*

> Specifies the class name of the Java code to be executed.

codebase=*url*

> Specifies the base URL for the application.

Navigator only

border=*number*

> Specifies the width of the border (in pixels) around the media object.

frameborder=yes|no

> Turns the border on or off.

pluginurl=*url*

> Specifies a source for installing the appropriate plug-in for the media file. Navigator recommends that you use pluginurl instead of pluginspage.

type=*MIME type*

> Specifies the MIME type of the plug-in needed to run the file. Navigator uses either the value of the type attribute or the suffix of the filename given as the source to determine which plug-in to use.

<fieldset>   `<fieldset> ... </fieldset>`

NN: 2, 3, 4 · MSIE: 2, 3, 4, 5 · HTML 4 · WebTV · Opera3

Used in forms, `<fieldset>` groups related controls and labels. The proper use of this tag should make documents more accessible to nonvisual browsers. It is similar to `<div>` but is specifically for grouping fields.

<font>   `<font>...</font>`

NN: 2, 3, 4 · MSIE: 2, 3, 4, 5 · HTML 4[D] · WebTV · Opera3

Used to affect the style (color, typeface, and size) of the enclosed text. This tag is deprecated in the HTML 4.0 Specification in favor of style sheet controls.

Attributes

color=*#rrggbb*
> Specifies the color using a hexadecimal RGB value.

face=*typeface* (or *list of typefaces*)
> Specifies a typeface for the text. The specified typeface will be used only if it is found on the user's machine. When a list of fonts (separated by commas) is specified, the browser will use the first available in the string.

size=1|2|3|4|5|6|7|+1|+2|+3|+4|-1|-2
> Sets the size of the type to an absolute value on a scale from 1 to 7 (3 is the default), or using a relative value +n or -n (based on the default or `<basefont>` setting).

<form>   `<form> ... </form>`

NN: 2, 3, 4 · MSIE: 2, 3, 4, 5 · HTML 4 · WebTV · Opera3

Indicates the beginning and end of a form. There can be more than one form in an HTML document; however, forms cannot be nested and it is important that they do not overlap.

Attributes

action=*url*

> Specifies the URL of the application that will process the form (required). This is most often a pointer to a CGI script on the server. The default is the current URL.

enctype=*encoding*

> Specifies how the values for the form controls are encoded when they are submitted to the server. The default is the Internet Media Type (application/x-www-form-urlencoded). The value multi-part/form-data should be used in combination with the file input element.

method=get|post

> Specifies which HTTP method will be used to submit the form data (required). With get (the default), the information is appended to and sent along with the URL itself. The post method puts the form information in a separate part of the body of the HTTP request. post is the preferred method according to the W3C specification.

HTML 4.0 Specification attributes

accept=content-type-list

> Specifies a comma-separated list of file types (MIME types) the server will accept and is able to process. Browsers may one day be able to filter out unacceptable files when prompting a user to upload files to the server.

accept-charset=*charset list*

> Specifies the list of character encodings (i.e., iso-8859-1) for input data that must be accepted by the server in order to process the current form. The value is a space-and/or comma-delimited list of charset values. The default value is unknown.

<frame>

Internet Explorer 3.0 and higher only

```
target=_blank|_top|_parent|_self
```
Specifies a target window for the results of the form submission to be loaded.

<frame>
<frame>

NN: 2, 3, 4 · MSIE: 2, 3, 4, 5 · HTML 4 · WebTV · Opera3

Defines a single frame within a <frameset>.

Attributes

```
bordercolor=#rrggbb or color name
```
Sets the color for frame's borders (if the border is turned
on). Support for this attribute is limited to Navigator 3.0
and higher and Internet Explorer 4.0.

```
frameborder=1|0
```
(Internet Explorer 3+ and W3C 4.0
Spec.); yes|no (Navigator 3+ and Internet Explorer
4.0)

Determines whether there is a 3–D separator drawn
between the current frame and surrounding frames. A
value of 1 (or yes) turns the border on. A value of 0 (or
no) turns the border off. You may also set the frameborder at the frameset level, which may be more
reliable.

Because Navigator and Internet Explorer support different values, you may need to specify the frameborder
twice within <frame> to ensure full browser compatibility, as follows:

```
frameborder=yes frameborder=1 ...
```
```
longdesc=url
```
Specifies a link to a document containing a long description of the frame and its contents. This addition to the
HTML 4.0 Specification may be useful for non-visual
web browsers.

---

marginwidth=*number*

Specifies the amount of space (in pixels) between the left and right edges of the frame and its contents. The minimum value according to the HTML Specification is 1 pixel. Setting the value to 0 (zero) in order to place objects flush against the edge of the frame will work in Internet Explorer, however, Navigator will still display a 1-pixel margin space.

marginheight=*number*

Specifies the amount of space (in pixels) between the top and bottom edge of the frame and its contents. The minimum value according to the HTML Specification is 1 pixel. Setting the value to 0 (zero) in order to place objects flush against the edge of the frame will work in Internet Explorer, however, Navigator will still display a 1-pixel margin space.

name=*text*

Assigns a name to the frame. By using this name with the target attribute in a link, content can be directed to a specific frame.

noresize

Prevents users from resizing the frame. By default, despite specific frame size settings, users can resize a frame by clicking and dragging its borders.

scrolling=yes|no|auto

Specifies whether scrollbars appear in the frame. A value of yes mean scrollbars always appear; a value of no means scrollbars never appear; a value of auto (the default) means scrollbars appear automatically when the contents do not fit within the frame.

src=*url*

Specifies the location of the initial HTML file to be displayed by the frame.

<frameset>

<frameset>   <frameset>...</frameset>

NN: 2, 3, 4 · MSIE: 2, 3, 4, 5 · HTML 4 · WebTV · Opera3

Defines a collection of frames or other framesets.

Attributes

border=*number*

Sets frame border thickness (in pixels) between all the frames in a frameset (when the frame border is turned on). This attribute is not part of the W3C HTML Specification, however, it is supported by most browsers.

bordercolor=*#rrggbb* or *color name*

Sets a border color for all the borders in a frameset. Support for this attribute is limited to Navigator 3.0 and higher and Internet Explorer 4.0.

cols=*list* (*number, percentage,* or ***)

Establishes the number and sizes of columns in a frameset. The number of columns is determined by the number of values in the list. Size specifications can be in absolute pixel values, percentage values, or relative values (*) based on available space.

frameborder= 1|0 (Internet Explorer 3+ and W3C 4.0 Spec.); yes|no (Navigator 3+ and Internet Explorer 4.0)

Determines whether 3-D separators are drawn between frames in the frameset. A value of 1 (or yes) turns the borders on; 0 (or no) turns the borders off.

Because Navigator and Internet Explorer support different values, you may need to specify the frameborder twice within <frame> to ensure backwards compatibility, as follows:

frameborder=yes frameborder=1 ...

framespacing=*number*

Internet Explorer 3.0 and higher only. Adds additional space (in pixels) between adjacent frames.

---

rows=*list* (*number, percentage,* or *)

Establishes the number and sizes of rows in the frameset. The number of rows is determined by the number of values in the list. Size specifications can be in absolute pixel values, percentage values, or relative values (*) based on available space.

<h1> through <h6>   `<h1>...</h1>`

NN: 2, 3, 4 · MSIE: 2, 3, 4, 5 · HTML 4 · WebTV · Opera3

Specifies that the enclosed text is a heading. There are six different levels of headings, from <h1> to <h6>, with each subsequent level displaying at a smaller size. <h5> and <h6> usually display smaller than the surrounding body text.

Attributes

align=center|left|right

Used to align the header left, right, or centered on the page. Internet Explorer 3.0 and earlier do not support right alignment.

<head>   `<head>...</head>`

NN: 2, 3, 4 · MSIE: 2, 3, 4, 5 · HTML 4 · WebTV · Opera3

Defines the head (also called "header") portion of the document that contains information about the document. The <head> tag has no attributes, but serves only as a container for other header tags, such as <base>, <meta>, and <title>.

<hr>   `<hr>`

NN: 2, 3, 4 · MSIE: 2, 3, 4, 5 · HTML 4 · WebTV · Opera3

Adds a horizontal rule to the page.

Attributes

`align=center|left|right`

> If the rule is shorter than the width of the window, this tag controls horizontal alignment of the rule. The default is `center`.

`noshade`

> This displays the rule as a solid (non-shaded) bar.

`size=number`

> Specifies the thickness of the rule in pixels.

`width=number` (pixels or percentage)

> Specifies the length of the rule in pixels or as a percentage of the page width. By default, rules are the full width of the browser window.

<html>   `<html>...</html>`

NN: 2, 3, 4 · MSIE: 2, 3, 4, 5 · HTML 4 · WebTV · Opera3

Placed at the beginning and end of the document, this tag tells the browser that the entire document is composed in HTML.

<i>   `<i>...</i>`

NN: 2, 3, 4 · MSIE: 2, 3, 4, 5 · HTML 4 · WebTV · Opera3

Enclosed text is displayed in italic.

<iframe>   `<iframe> ... </iframe>`

NN: 2, 3, 4 · MSIE: 2, 3, 4, 5 · HTML 4 · WebTV · Opera3

Defines a floating frame within a document with similar placement tags to `<img>`. This element requires a closing tag. Introduced by Internet Explorer 3.0, inline frames are now part of the W3C HTML 4.0 Specification. As of this writing, however, they are only supported by Internet Explorer.

Attributes

align=top|middle|bottom|left|right

Aligns the inline frame on the page within the flow of the text. Left and right alignment allows text to flow around the frame.

frameborder=1|0

Turns on or off the displaying of a 3–D border for the frame. The default is 1, which inserts the border.

height=*number*

Specifies the height of the frame in pixels or as a percentage of the window size.

hspace=*number*

Used in conjunction with left and right alignment, this attribute specifies the amount of space (in pixels) to hold clear to the left and right of the frame.

marginheight=*number*

Specifies the amount of space (in pixels) between the top and bottom edges of the frame and its contents.

marginwidth=*number*

Specifies the amount of space (in pixels) between the left and right edges of the frame and its contents.

name=*text*

Assigns a name to the inline frame to be referenced by targeted links.

noresize

Prevents users from resizing the inline frame. By default, despite specific frame size settings, users can resize a frame by clicking and dragging its borders.

scrolling=yes|no|auto

Determines whether scrollbars appear in the frame (see explanation in <frame> above).

src=*url*

Specifies the URL of the HTML document that will initially display in the frame.

vspace=*number*

> Used in conjunction with left and right alignment, this attribute specifies the amount of space (in pixels) to hold clear above and below the frame.

width=*number*

> Specifies the width of the frame in pixels or as a percentage of the window size.

<img>

NN: 2, 3, 4 · MSIE: 2, 3, 4, 5 · HTML 4 · WebTV · Opera3

Places a graphic on the page.

Attributes

align=*type* (see options below)

> Specifies the alignment of an image using one of the following values:

Type	Resulting Alignment
absbottom	*Navigator 3.0/4.0 and Internet Explorer 4.0 only.* Aligns the bottom of the image with the bottom of the current line.
absmiddle	*Navigator 3.0/4.0 and Internet Explorer 4.0 only.* Aligns the middle of the image with the middle of the current line.
baseline	*Navigator 3.0/4.0 and Internet Explorer 4.0 only.* Aligns the bottom of the image with the baseline of the current line.
bottom	Aligns the bottom of the image with the text baseline. This is the default vertical alignment.
center	According to the W3C HTML 4.0 Specification, this centers the image horizontally on the page; however, in reality, browsers treat it the same as align=middle.

Type	Resulting Alignment
`left`	Aligns image on the left margin and allows subsequent text to wrap around it.
`middle`	Aligns the text baseline with the middle of the image.
`right`	Aligns image on the right margin and allows subsequent text to wrap around it.
`texttop`	*Navigator only*. Aligns the top of the image with the ascenders of the text line.
`top`	Aligns the top of the image with the top of the tallest object on that line.

`alt=`*text*

Provides a string of alternative text that appears when the image is not displayed.

`border=`*number*

Specifies the width (in pixels) of the border that surrounds a linked image. It is standard practice to set `border=0` to turn the border off.

`height=`*number*

Specifies the height of the image in pixels. It is not required, but recommended to speed up the rendering of the web page.

`hspace=`*number*

Used in conjunction with the `align` attribute, this attribute specifies in number of pixels the amount of space to leave clear to the left and right of the image.

`ismap`

Indicates that the graphic is used as the basis for a server-side imagemap (an image containing multiple hypertext links).

`longdesc=`*url*

New in HTML 4.0 Specification. Specifies a link to a long description of the image or an imagemap's contents.

<img>

This is used to make information about the image accessible to nonvisual browsers.

lowsrc=*url*

Navigator (all versions) and Internet Explorer 4.0 only.
Specifies an image (usually of a smaller file size) that will download first, followed by the final image specified by the src attribute.

src=*url*

Provides the URL of the graphic file to be displayed.

usemap=*url*

Specifies the map containing coordinates and links for a client-side imagemap (an image containing multiple hypertext links).

vspace=*number*

Used in conjunction with the align attribute, this attribute specifies (in pixels) the amount of space to leave clear above and below the image.

width=*number*

Specifies the width of the image in pixels. It is not required, but recommended to speed up the rendering of the web page.

Internet Explorer's DYNSRC attribute

Internet Explorer versions 2.0 and later use the <img> tag to place a video on the page using the dynsrc attribute. The following attributes are related to the dynsrc function and work only with Internet Explorer:

controls

Adds playback controls for the video.

dynsrc=*url*

Provides the URL for the video file to be displayed on the page.

`loop=`*`number`*`|infinite`

> Sets the number of times to play the video. It can be a number value or set to infinite.

`start=fileopen|mouseover`

> Specifies when to play the video. By default, it begins playing as soon as it's downloaded (`fileopen`). You can set it to start when the mouse pointer is over the movie area (`mouseover`). If you combine them (separated by a comma), the movie plays once it is downloaded, then again every time the user mouses over it.

\<input type=button\>   `<input type=button>`

NN: 2, 3, 4 · MSIE: 2, 3, 4, 5 · HTML 4 · WebTV · Opera3

Within a `<form>`, creates a customizable "push" button. Customizable buttons have no specific behavior but can be used to trigger functions created with JavaScript controls.

Attributes

`name=`*`text`*

> Assigns a name to the form element to be passed to the forms processing application.

`value=`*`text`*

> Specifies the initial value for the parameter.

\<input type=checkbox\>   `<input type=checkbox>`

NN: 2, 3, 4 · MSIE: 2, 3, 4, 5 · HTML 4 · WebTV · Opera3

Creates a checkbox input element within a `<form>`. Checkboxes are like on/off switches that can be toggled by the user. When a form is submitted, only the "on" checkboxes submit values to the server. Any number of checkboxes may be selected within a form.

<input type=file>

Attributes

checked

> When this attribute is added, the checkbox will be checked by default.

name=*text*

> Assigns a name to the checkbox to be passed to the form-processing application if selected. Giving several checkboxes the same name creates a group of checkbox elements, allowing users to select several options with the same property.

value=*text*

> Specifies the initial value of the control that is passed on to the server. If not defined, a value of "on" is sent.

<input type=file>   <input type=file>

NN: 2, 3, 4 · MSIE: 2, 3, 4, 5 · HTML 4 · WebTV · Opera3

Within a <form>, allows users to submit external files with their form submission. It is accompanied by a "browse" button when displayed in the browser.

Attributes

accept=*MIME type*

> Specifies a comma-separated list of content types that a server processing the form will handle correctly. It can be used to filter out nonconforming files when prompting a user to select files to send to the server.

name=*text*

> Assigns a name to the control.

value=*text*

> Specifies the initial filename to be submitted.

<input type=hidden>   `<input type=hidden>`

NN: 2, 3, 4 · MSIE: 2, 3, 4, 5 · HTML 4 · WebTV · Opera3

Within a `<form>`, creates an element that does not display in the browser. Hidden controls can be used to pass special form-processing information along to the server that the user cannot see or alter.

Attributes

`name=text`

> Specifies the name of the parameter that is passed to the form-processing application for this input element (required).

`value=text`

> Specifies the value of the element that is passed to the form-processing application.

<input type=image>   `<input type=image>`

NN: 2, 3, 4 · MSIE: 2, 3, 4, 5 · HTML 4 · WebTV · Opera3

Within a `<form>`, allows an image to be used as a substitute for a `submit` button.

Attributes

`align=top|middle|bottom`

> Aligns the image with respect to the surrounding text lines.

`name=text`

> Specifies the name of the parameter to be passed along to the form-processing application.

`src=url`

> Provides the URL of the image (required).

<input type=radio>

<input type=password>　　　　　<input type=password>

NN: 2, 3, 4 · MSIE: 2, 3, 4, 5 · HTML 4 · WebTV · Opera3

Within a <form>, creates a text-input element (like text) but the input text is rendered in a way that hides the characters, such as displaying a string of asterisks (*) or bullets (•). Note this does not encrypt the information and should not be considered as a real security measure.

Attributes

maxlength=*number*

Specifies the maximum number of characters the user can input for this element.

name=*text*

Specifies the name of this parameter to be passed to the form-processing application for this element (required).

size=*number*

Specifies the size of the text-entry box (measured in number of characters) to be displayed for this element. Users can type entries that are longer than the space provided, causing the field to scroll to the right.

value=*text*

Specifies the value that will initially be displayed in the text box.

<input type=radio>　　　　　<input type=radio>

NN: 2, 3, 4 · MSIE: 2, 3, 4, 5 · HTML 4 · WebTV · Opera3

Within a <form>, creates a radio button that can be turned on and off. When a group of radio buttons share the same control name, only one button within the group can be "on" at one time and all the others will be turned "off." This makes them different from checkboxes, which allow multiple choices to be selected within a group.

<input type=radio>

Attributes

checked

Causes the radio button to be in the "on" state when the form is initially displayed.

name=*text*

Specifies the name of the parameter to be passed to the forms-processing application if this element is selected (required).

value=*text*

Specifies the value of the parameter to be passed on to the forms-processing application.

`<input type=reset>` <input type=reset>

NN: 2, 3, 4 · MSIE: 2, 3, 4, 5 · HTML 4 · WebTV · Opera3

Within a <form>, creates a reset button that clears the contents (or sets them to their default values) of the elements in a form.

Attributes

value=*text*

Specifies alternate text to appear in the button (default text is "Reset").

`<input type=submit>` <input type=submit>

NN: 2, 3, 4 · MSIE: 2, 3, 4, 5 · HTML 4 · WebTV · Opera3

Within a <form>, creates a submit button that sends the information in the form to the server for processing.

Attributes

value=*text*

Specifies alternate text to appear in the button (default text is "Submit").

<ins>

`<input type=text>` `<input type=text>`

NN: 2, 3, 4 · MSIE: 2, 3, 4, 5 · HTML 4 · WebTV · Opera3

Within a `<form>`, creates a text input element. This is the default input type; using the `<input>` tag without a type attribute creates a text input element.

Attributes

`maxlength=number`

Specifies the maximum number of characters the user can input for this element.

`name=text`

Specifies the name of this parameter to be passed to the form-processing application for this element (required).

`size=number`

Specifies the size of the text-entry box (measured in number of characters) to be displayed for this element. Users can type entries that are longer than the space provided, causing the field to scroll to the right.

`value=text`

Specifies the value that will initially be displayed in the text box.

`<ins>` `<ins>...</ins>`

NN: 2, 3, 4 · MSIE: 2, 3, 4, 5 · HTML 4 · WebTV · Opera3

Indicates text that has been inserted into the document. It has no inherent style qualities on its own, but may be used to indicate inserted text in a different color via style sheet controls. It may be useful for legal documents and any instance in which edits need to be tracked. Its counterpart is `<del>` (deleted text). Both can be used to indicate either inline or block-level elements.

<isindex>

<isindex> <isindex>

NN: 2, 3, 4 · MSIE: 2, 3, 4, 5 · HTML 4D · WebTV · Opera3

An early and outdated way of searching a document, this tag marks the document as searchable. <isindex> requires that the system serving the doucment be running a compatible search engine. The server on which the document is located must have a search engine that supports this searching. The browser will display a text entry field and a generic line that says, "This is a searchable index. Enter search keywords."

<kbd> <kbd>...</kbd>

NN: 2, 3, 4 · MSIE: 2, 3, 4, 5 · HTML 4 · WebTV · Opera3

Indicates text that is typed on a keyboard. It is displayed in the browser's monospace font (usually Courier). Some browsers also display it in bold.

<keygen> <keygen>...</keygen>

NN: 2, 3, 4 · MSIE: 2, 3, 4, 5 · HTML 4 · WebTV · Opera3

An early attempt by Navigator at making forms submissions secure.

Attributes

challenge=*string*

   Specifies the challenge string to be packaged with the public key in the PublicKeyAndChallenge for use in verification of the form submission. If no challenge string is provided, it is encoded as an IA5STRING of length zero.

name=*text*

   Specifies the name for the element.

<layer>

\<label>   `<label>...</label>`

NN: 2, 3, 4 · **MSIE: 2, 3, 4, 5** · **HTML 4** – WebTV · Opera3

Used to attach information to form controls. Each `label`
element is associated with exactly one form control.

Attributes

for=*text*

> Explicitly associates the label with the control by match-
> ing the value of the `for` attribute with the value of the
> `id` attribute within the control element.

Example

```
<LABEL for="lastname">Last Name: </LABEL>
<INPUT type="text" id="lastname" size="32">
```

\<layer>   `<layer>...</layer>`

NN: 2, **3, 4** · MSIE: 2, 3, 4, 5 · HTML 4 · WebTV · Opera3

Navigator only. Originally introduced by Netscape to identify distinct content objects as part of Netscape's DHTML
implementation. Use of the `<layer>` tag is discouraged, in
favor of Cascading Sytle Sheets with Positioning; in reality,
the `<layer>` tag is required for rendering DHTML pages for
Navigator 4.0.

Attributes

above=*layer name*

> Identifies the layer immediately above (in stacking
> order) the newly created layer. The named layer must
> already exist.

background=*url(filename)*

> Specifies an image to be used as the background.

be1ow=*layer name*

Identifies the layer immediately below the newly created layer. The named layer must already exist.

bgco1or=*#rrggbb* or *color name*

Specifies the background color of the layer.

c1ip=*n,n,n,n*

Defines the boundaries of the clipping rectangle (visible area) of the layer.

The value is a set of four numbers, indicating in order, the left value, the top value, the right value and the bottom value. The left and right values are specified as pixels in from the left, while the top and bottom values are specified as pixels down from the origin of the layer.

height=*number, percentage*

Specifies the height of the layer.

id=*text*

Specifies the layer's ID, so it can be referenced by other layers and JavaScript.

1eft=*number*

Specifies the absolute horizontal position of the layer. The setting 1eft=50 would position the layer 50 pixels from the left edge of the window.

name=*text*

Specifies the name of the layer so that it can be referenced by other layers and JavaScript.

pagex=*number*

Specifies the horizontal position of the layer relative to the document's window.

pagey=*number*

Specifies the vertical position of the layer relative to the document's window.

src=*url*

Specifies an HTML document to be used in the layer.

top=*number*
> Specifies the absolute vertical position of the top edge of the layer. A setting of top=100 would place the layer 100 pixels from the top edge.

visibility=show|hide|inherit
> Determines whether the layer is visible. show makes the layer visible. hide makes it invisible. inherit causes the layer to have the same visibility as its parent layer.

width=*number, percentage*
> Specifies the width of the layer and determines how its contents wrap.

z-index=*number*
> Specifies the stacking order of a layer. Layers with higher z-index values are stacked above those with lower ones.

<legend>   <legend>...</legend>

NN: 2, 3, 4 · MSIE: 2, 3, 4, 5 · HTML 4 · WebTV · Opera3

Used in forms, this tag assigns a caption to a <fieldset>. This improves accessibility when the fieldset is rendered in non-visual browsers.

<li>   <li>...</li>

NN: 2, 3, 4 · MSIE: 2, 3, 4, 5 · HTML 4 · WebTV · Opera3

Defines an item in a list. It is used within the <dir>, <ol>, and <ul> list tags.

Attributes

The following attributes have been deprecated by the HTML 4.0 Specification in favor of style sheet controls for list item display.

---

type=*format*

> Changes the format of the automatically generated numbers or bullets for list items.

> Within unordered lists (<ul>), the type attribute can be used to specify the bullet style (disc, circle, or square) for a particular list item.

> Within ordered lists (<ol>), the type attribute specifies the numbering style (see options under <ol> listing below) for a particular list item.

value=*number*

> Within ordered lists, you can specify the number that appears next to an item. Following list items will increase from the specified number.

<link>

<link>

NN: 2, 3, 4 · MSIE: 2, 3, 4, 5 · HTML 4 · WebTV · Opera3

Defines a relationship between the current document and another document. This tag goes within the <head> portion of the document. It is often used to refer to an external stylesheet.

Attributes

href=*url*

> Identifies the target document.

methods=*list*

> Specifies a browser-dependent list of comma-separated display methods for this link. It is not commonly used.

rel=*relationship* (such as toc, glossary, or parent)

> Specifies the relationship of the current source document to the target. For example, rel=stylesheet is used to create a relationship with an external stylesheet.

rel=stylesheet

> This attribute is used within the <link> tag to create a relationship with an external stylesheet.

---

rev=*relationship* (such as toc, glossary, or parent)

Specifies the relationship of the target document to the source.

title=*text*

Provides a title for the target document.

type=*MIME-Type*

Shows the type of an outside link. The value text/css indicates that the linked document is an external cascading style sheet.

urn=*urn*

Defines a location-independent Universal Resource Name (URN) for the referenced document. The actual syntax of the URN has not been defined, making this essentially a placeholder for future versions of HTML.

\<map>   \<map>...\</map>

NN: 2, 3, 4 · MSIE: 2, 3, 4, 5 · HTML 4 · WebTV · Opera3

Encloses client-side imagemap specifications. See the tag structure section "Client-side Imagemaps" in this reference for more information.

Attributes

name=*text*

Gives the imagemap a name that is then referenced within the \<img> tag. This attribute is required.

\<marquee>   \<marquee>...\</marquee>

NN: 2, 3, 4 · MSIE: 2, 3, 4, 5 · HTML 4 · WebTV · Opera3

Creates a scrolling-text marquee area.

Attributes

align=top|middle|bottom

Aligns the marquee with the top, middle, or bottom of the neighboring text line.

`behavior=scroll|slide|alternate`

Specifies how the text should behave. `scroll` is the default setting and means the text should start completely off one side, scroll all the way across and completely off, then start over again. `slide` stops the scroll when the text touches the other margin. `alternate` means bounce back and forth within the marquee.

`bgcolor=#rrggbb` or `color name`

Sets background color of marquee.

`direction=left|right`

Defines the direction in which the text scrolls.

`height=number`

Defines the height in pixels of the marquee area.

`hspace=number`

Holds a number of pixels space clear to the left and right of the marquee.

`loop=number|infinite`

Specifies the number of loops as a number value or infinite.

`scrollamount=number`

Sets the number of pixels to move the text for each scroll movement.

`scrolldelay=number`

Specifies the delay, in milliseconds, between successive movements of the marquee text.

`vspace=number`

Holds a number of pixels space clear above and below the marquee.

`width=number`

Specifies the width in pixels of the marquee.

<meta>

<meta> <meta>

NN: 2, 3, 4 · MSIE: 2, 3, 4, 5 · HTML 4 · WebTV · Opera3

Provides additional information about the document. It
should be placed within the <head> tags at the beginning
of the document. It is commonly used for improving a document's searchability (by adding keywords) and may be
used for rudimentary push functions.

Attributes

content=*text*

> Specifies the value of the meta tag and is always used in
> conjunction with name or http-equiv.

http-equiv=*text*

> Specifies information to be included in the HTTP head-
> er that the server appends to the document. It is used in
> conjunction with the name attribute.

name=*text*

> Specifies a name for the meta information.

scheme=*text*

> Provides additional information for the interpretation of
> metadata. This is a new attribute introduced in HTML
> 4.0.

Example

The http-equiv attribute is used to automatically load
pages at timed intervals using the following syntax:

```
<META http-eqiv="refresh" content="1;
url=http://www.oreilly.com">
```

where the number equals the delay in seconds and the value of url is the URL to be loaded.

<menu>

<menu>...</menu>

NN: 2, 3, 4ᴰ · MSIE: 2, 3, 4, 5 · HTML 4ᴰ · WebTV · Opera3

This indicates the beginning and end of a menu list, which consists of list items <li>. A menu list is intended to be used for short choices, such as a list of links to other documents. It is little used and has been deprecated in favor of <ul>.

Attributes

compact

> Displays the list as small as possible (not many browsers do anything with this attribute).

type=disc|circle|square

> Defines the shape of the bullets used for each list item.

<multicol>

<multicol>...</multicol>

NN: 2, 3, 4 · MSIE: 2, 3, 4, 5 · HTML 4 · WebTV · Opera3

Navigator only. Displays enclosed text in multiple columns of approximately the same length.

Attributes

cols=*number*

> Specifies the number of columns (required).

gutter=*number*

> Specifies the amount of space (in pixels) between columns.

width=*number*

> Specifies the width of the columns in pixels. All columns within <multicol> are the same width.

<nolayer>

<nobr>
<nobr>...</nobr>

NN: 2, 3, 4 · MSIE: 2, 3, 4, 5 · HTML 4 · WebTV · Opera3

Text (or graphics) within the "no break" tags will always display on one line, without allowing any breaks. The line may run beyond the right edge of the browser window, requiring horizontal scrolling.

<noembed>
<noembed>...</noembed>

NN: 2, 3, 4 · MSIE: 2, 3, 4, 5 · HTML 4 · WebTV · Opera3

The text or object specified by <noembed> will appear when an embedded object cannot be displayed (e.g., when the appropriate plug-in is not available). This tag is placed within the <embed> container tags.

<noframes>
<noframes> ... </noframes>

NN: 2, 3, 4 · MSIE: 2, 3, 4, 5 · HTML 4 · WebTV · Opera3

Defines content that will be displayed by browsers that cannot display frames. Browsers that do support frames will ignore the content between <noframes> tags.

<nolayer>
<nolayer> ... </nolayer>

NN: 2, 3, 4 · MSIE: 2, 3, 4, 5 · HTML 4 · WebTV · Opera3

Specifies content that will be ignored by Navigator, but will be displayed in all other browsers. It is used to display substitute content when layers are not supported.

<noscript>   <noscript>...</noscript>

NN: 2, 3, 4 · MSIE: 2, 3, 4, 5 · HTML 4 · WebTV · Opera3

Provides alternate content for browsers that are not enabled to run scripts (either because the browser does not recognize the <script> tag, or because it has been configured not to run scripts).

<object>   <object>...</object>

NN: 2, 3, 4 · **MSIE: 2, 3, 4, 5** · **HTML 4** · WebTV · Opera3

Places an object (such as an applet, media file, etc.) on a web page. It is similar to the <embed> tag. The <object> tag often contains information for retrieving ActiveX controls that Internet Explorer on Windows uses to display the object.

Attributes

align=baseline|center|left|middle|right|
   textbottom|textmiddle|texttop

Aligns object with respect to surrounding text.

border=*number*

Sets the width of the border in pixels if the object is a link.

classid=*url*

Identifies the class identifier of the object. The syntax depends on the object type.

codebase=*url*

Identifies the URL of the object's codebase. Syntax depends on the object.

codetype=*codetype*

Internet Explorer 3.0/4.0 and HTML 4.0 Specification only. Specifies the media type of the code. Examples of code types include `audio/basic`, `text/html`, and `image/gif`.

`data=`*url*

Specifies the URL of the data used for the object. The syntax depends on the object.

`declare`

Internet Explorer 3.0 and HTML 4.0 Specification only. Declares an object without instantiating it.

`height=`*number*

Specifies the height of the object in pixels.

`hspace=`*number*

Holds a number of pixels space clear to the left and right of the object.

`name=`*text*

Specifies the name of the object to be referenced by scripts on the page.

`shapes`

Internet Explorer 3.0 and HTML 4.0 Specification only. Indicates that the object contains an imagemap.

`standby=`*text message*

Internet Explorer 3.0 and HTML 4.0 Specification only. Specifies message to display during object loading.

`type=`*type*

Specifies the media type for the data.

`usemap=`*url*

Specifies the imagemap to use with the object.

`vspace=`*number*

Holds a number of pixels space clear above and below the object.

<ol>

\<ol\>

<ol>...</ol>

NN: 2, 3, 4 · MSIE: 2, 3, 4, 5 · HTML 4 · WebTV · Opera3

Defines the beginning and end of an ordered (numbered) list, which consists of list items <li>.

Attributes

compact

> Displays the list as small as possible (not many browsers do anything with this attribute).

start=*number*

> Starts the numbering of the list at the specified number, instead of 1.

type=1|A|a|I|i

> Defines the numbering system for the list as follows:

Type Value	Generated Style	Sample Sequence
1	Arabic numerals (default)	1, 2, 3, 4...
A	Uppercase letters	A, B, C, D...
a	Lowercase letters	a, b, c, d...
I	Uppercase Roman numerals	I, II, III, IV...
i	Lowercase Roman numerals	i, ii, iii, iv...

The type attribute has been deprecated by the HTML 4.0 Specification in favor of style sheet controls for list item display.

\<optgroup\>

<optgroup>...</optgroup>

NN: 2, 3, 4 · MSIE: 2, 3, 4, 5 · HTML 4 · WebTV · Opera3

Within the <select> form element, this tag defines a logical group of <option> tags. This could be used by browsers to display hierarchical cascading menus. <optgroup> tags cannot be nested.

Attributes

`label=`*text*

Specifies the label for the option group (required).

<option>   `<option> ... </option>`

NN: 2, 3, 4 · MSIE: 2, 3, 4, 5 · HTML 4 · WebTV · Opera3

Defines an option within a `<select>` form element (a multiple-choice menu or scrolling list). The end tag, although it exists, is usually omitted.

Attributes

`selected`

Makes this item selected when the form is initially displayed.

`value=`*text*

Returns a specified value to the forms-processing application instead of the `<option>` contents.

`width=`*number*

Specifies the object width in pixels.

<p>   `<p>...</p>`

NN: 2, 3, 4 · MSIE: 2, 3, 4, 5 · HTML 4 · WebTV · Opera3

Denotes the beginning and end of a paragraph when used as container. Many browsers will also allow the `<p>` tag to be used without a closing tag. The container method is preferred, particularly if you are using Cascading Style Sheets with the document.

Attributes

`align=center|left|right`

Aligns the text within the tags to the left, right, or center of the page.

<param>   <param>...</param>

NN: 2, 3, 4 · MSIE: 2, 3, 4, 5 · HTML 4 · WebTV · Opera3

Supplies a parameter within the <applet> or <object> tag.

Attributes

name=*text*

Defines the name of the parameter.

value=*text*

Defines the value of the parameter.

valuetype=data|ref|object

Internet Explorer only. Indicates the type of value: data indicates that the parameter's value is data (default); ref indicates that the parameter's value is a URL; object indicates that the value is the URL of another object in the document.

type=*type*

Internet Explorer only. Specifies the media type.

<pre>   <pre>...</pre>

NN: 2, 3, 4 · MSIE: 2, 3, 4, 5 · HTML 4 · WebTV · Opera3

Delimits preformatted text, meaning that lines are displayed exactly as they are typed in, honoring multiple spaces and line breaks. Text within <pre> tags will be displayed in a monospace font such as Courier.

Attributes

width=*number*

This optional attribute determines how many characters to fit on a single line within the <pre> block.

<q>   <q>...</q>

NN: 2, 3, 4 · MSIE: 2, 3, 4, 5 · HTML 4 · WebTV · Opera3

Delimits a short quotation that can be included inline, such as "to be or not to be." It differs from <blockquote>, which is for longer quotations set off as a separate paragraph element. It may be rendered with quotation marks.

Attributes

cite=*url*

Designates the source document from which the quotation was taken.

<s>   <s>...</s>

NN: 2, 3, 4 · MSIE: 2, 3, 4, 5 · HTML 4[D] · WebTV · Opera3

Enclosed text is displayed as strike-through text (same as <strike> but introduced by later browser versions).

<samp>   <samp>...</samp>

NN: 2, 3, 4 · MSIE: 2, 3, 4, 5 · HTML 4 · WebTV · Opera3

Delimits sample output from programs, scripts, etc. Sample text is generally displayed in a monospace font.

<script>   <script>...</script>

NN: 2, 3, 4 · MSIE: 2, 3, 4, 5 · HTML 4 · WebTV · Opera3

Adds a script that is to be used in the document.

Attributes

type=*content type*

Specifies the language of the script. Its value must be a media type (ex. text/javascript). This attribute is

---

required by the HTML 4.0 Specification and is a recommended replacement for the "language" attribute.

language=*language*

Identifies the language of the script, such as JavaScript or VBScript. This attribute has been deprecated by the HTML 4.0 Specification in favor of the type attribute.

src=*url*

Netscape only. Specifies the URL of an outside file containing the script to be loaded and run with the document.

<select>   <select> ... </select>

NN: 2, 3, 4 · MSIE: 2, 3, 4, 5 · HTML 4 · WebTV · Opera3

Defines a form element that can be a multiple-choice menu or a scrolling list. It is a container for one or more <option> tags.

Attributes

multiple

This allows the user to select more than one <option> from the list.

name=*text*

Defines the name for selected <option> values that, if selected, are passed on to the forms-processing application (required).

size=*number*

Controls the display of the list of options. When size=1 (and multiple is not specified), the list is displayed as a pull-down menu. For values higher than 1, the options are displayed as a scrolling list with the specified number of options visible.

\<server\>   `<server>...</server>`

NN: 2, 3, 4 · MSIE: 2, 3, 4, 5 · HTML 4 · WebTV · Opera3

Specifies server-side JavaScript statements that are compiled by LiveWire.

\<small\>   `<small>...</small>`

NN: 2, 3, 4 · **MSIE: 2,** 3, **4, 5** · **HTML 4** · **WebTV** · **Opera3**

Renders the type one font size smaller than the surrounding text. It is equivalent to `<font size="-1">`.

\<spacer\>   `<spacer>`

NN: 2, 3, 4 · MSIE: 2, 3, 4, 5 · HTML 4 · **WebTV** · Opera3

Holds a specified amount of blank space within the flow of a page. It is often used to maintain space within table cells for correct display in Navigator.

Attributes

`type=vertical|horizontal|block`

> Specifies the type of spacer: `vertical` inserts space between two lines of text, `horizontal` inserts space between characters, and `block` inserts a rectangular space.

`size=`*number*

> Specifies a number of pixels to be used with a vertical or horizontal spacer.

`height=`*number*

> Specifies height in number of pixels for a block spacer.

`width=`*number*

> Specifies width in pixels for a `block` spacer.

`align=`*`value`*

> Aligns `block` spacer with surrounding text. Values are the same as for the `<img>` tag.

<span> <span style="float:right">`<span>...</span>`</span>

NN: 2, 3, 4 · MSIE: 2, 3, 4, 5 · HTML 4 · WebTV · Opera3

This is a null text container used for identifying a span of inline characters. It has no inherent style effect on its own, but can be used in conjunction with Cascading Style Sheets to apply styles to any span of text.

<strike> <span style="float:right">`<strike>...</strike>`</span>

NN: 2, 3, 4 · MSIE: 2, 3, 4, 5 · HTML 4D · WebTV · Opera3

Enclosed text is displayed as strike-through text (crossed through with a horizontal line).

<strong> <span style="float:right">`<strong>...</strong>`</span>

NN: 2, 3, 4 · MSIE: 2, 3, 4, 5 · HTML 4 · WebTV · Opera3

Enclosed text is strongly emphasized. Nearly all browsers render `<strong>` text in bold.

<sub> <span style="float:right">`<sub>...</sub>`</span>

NN: 2, 3, 4 · MSIE: 2, 3, 4, 5 · HTML 4 · WebTV · Opera3

Formats enclosed text as subscript.

<sup> <span style="float:right">`<sup>...</sup>`</span>

NN: 2, 3, 4 · MSIE: 2, 3, 4, 5 · HTML 4 · WebTV · Opera3

Formats enclosed text as superscript.

<table>

\<table\>   \<table\>...\</table\>

NN: 2, 3, 4 · MSIE: 2, 3, 4, 5 · HTML 4 · WebTV · Opera3

Defines the beginning and end of a table. The end tag is
required, and its omission may cause the table not to ren-
der in some browsers.

Attribute

align=left|right|center

Aligns the table within the text flow (same as align in
the \<img\> tag). The default alignment is left. The cen-
ter value is not universally supported, so it is more
reliable to center a table on a page using tags outside
the table (such as \<center\> or \<div\>). This attribute
has been deprecated by the W3C HTML 4.0 Specifica-
tion in favor of style sheet positioning.

background=*url*

Specifies a graphic image to be tiled in the background
of the table. In Internet Explorer 3.0 and higher, the
image tiles behind the entire table. In Navigator 4.0, the
tile repeats in each individual frame (although its sup-
port is not officially documented).

bgcolor=*#rrggbb* or *color name*

Specifies a background color for the entire table. Value
is specified in hexadecimal RGB values or by color
name.

border=*number*

Specifies the width (in pixels) of the border around the
table and its cells. Set it to border=0 to turn the bor-
ders off completely. The default value is 1. Adding the
word border without a value results in a 1-pixel border.

cellpadding=*number*

Sets the amount of space inside the cell, in number of
pixels, between the cellborder and its contents. The
default value is 1.

cellspacing=*number*

    Sets the amount of space (in number of pixels) between table cells. The default value is 2.

frame=void|above|below|hsides|lhs|rhs|
    vsides|box|border

    Tells the browser where to draw borders around the table. The values are as follows:

void

    The frame does not appear (default)

above

    Top side only

below

    Bottom side only

hsides

    Top and bottom sides only

vsides

    Right and left sides only

lhs

    Left-hand side only

rhs

    Right-hand side only

box

    All four sides

border

    All four sides

    When the border attribute is set to a value greater than zero, the frame defaults to border unless otherwise specified. This attribute was introduced by Internet Explorer 3.0 and now appears in the HTML 4.0 Specification. It is not supported by Navigator as of this writing.

height=*number, percentage*

    Specifies the height of the entire table. It can be specified in a specific number of pixels or by a percentage of the browser window.

`hspace=`*number*

> Holds a number of pixels space to the left and right of an aligned table (same as hspace in the <img> tag).

`rules=none|groups|rows|cols|all`

> Tells the browser where to draw rules within the table. Its values are as follows:

`none`
> No rules (default)

`groups`
> Rules appear between row groups (thead, tfoot, and tbody) and column groups

`rows`
> Rules appear between rows only

`cols`
> Rules appear between columns only

`all`
> Rules appear between all rows and columns

> When the border attribute is set to a value greater than zero, rules default to all unless otherwise specified.

> This attribute was introduced by Internet Explorer 3.0 and now appears in the HTML 4.0 Specification. It is not supported by Navigator as of this writing.

`summary=`*text*

> Provides a summary of the table contents for use with non-visual browsers.

`vspace=`*number*

> Holds a number of pixels space above and below an aligned table (same as vspace in the <img> tag).

`width=`*number, percentage*

> Specifies the width of the entire table. It can be specified in a specific number of pixels or by percentage of the browser window.

Internet Explorer 2.0 and higher only

bordercolor=*#rrggbb* or *color name*

Specifies the color of the main center portion of a table border. (Table borders are rendered using three color values to create a 3–D effect.)

bordercolorlight=*#rrggbb* or *color name*

Specifies the color of the light shade used to render 3–D table borders.

bordercolordark=*#rrggbb* or *color name*

Specifies the color of the dark shade used to render 3–D table borders.

<tbody>   <tbody>...</tbody>

NN: 2, 3, 4 · MSIE: 2, 3, 4, 5 · HTML 4 · WebTV · Opera3

Within a <table>, defines a row or group of rows as the "body" of the table. It must contain at least one row (<tr>). The end tag is optional.

"Row group" tags (tbody, thead, and tfoot) were introduced by Internet Explorer and are part of the HTML 4.0 Specification, but all attributes may not be fully supported. The system could speed table display and provide a mechanism for scrolling the body of a table independently of its head and foot. It could also be useful for printing long tables for which the head information could be printed on each page.

Attributes

align=left|center|right|justify|char

Specifies horizontal alignment (or justification) of cell contents.

char=*character*

Specifies a character along which the cell contents will be aligned. The default character is a decimal point (language-appropriate).

---

charoff=*length*

> Specifies the distance to the first alignment character (char) on each line. If a line doesn't use an alignment character, it should be horizontally shifted to end at the alignment position.

valign=top|middle|bottom|baseline

> Specifies vertical alignment of cell contents.

<td>

<td>...</td>

NN: 2, 3, 4 · MSIE: 2, 3, 4, 5 · HTML 4 · WebTV · Opera3

Within a <table>, defines a table data cell. The end tag is not required, but may prevent unpredictable table display, particularly if the cell contains images. A table cell can contain any content, including another table.

Attributes

align=left|center|right

> Aligns the text (or other elements) within the table cell. The default value is left. This attribute has been deprecated by the W3C HTML 4.0 Specification in favor of positioning with style sheets.

background=*url*

> Specifies a graphic image to be used as a tile within the cell. Navigator's documentation does not cover this tag, but it is supported by version 4.0.

bgcolor=#*rrggbb* or *color name*

> Specifies a color to be used in the table cell. A cell's background color overrides colors specified at the row or table levels.

colspan=*number*

> Specifies the number of columns the current cell should span. The default value is 1. According to the W3C HTML 4.0 Specification, the value 0 (zero) means the current cell spans all columns from the current column

---

<td>

to the last column in the table; in reality, however, this feature is not supported in currently available 4.0 browsers.

height=*number, percentage*

Specifies the height of the cell in number of pixels or by a percentage value relative to the table height. The height specified in the first column will apply to the rest of the cells in the row. The height values need to be consistent for cells in a particular row. This attribute has been deprecated in the W3C HTML 4.0 Specification.

nowrap

Disables automatic text wrapping for the current cell. Line breaks must be added with a <p> or <br>. This attribute has been deprecated by the W3C HTML 4.0 Specification in favor of style sheet controls.

rowspan=*number*

Specifies the number of rows spanned by the current cell. The default value is 1. According to the W3C HTML 4.0 Specification, the value 0 (zero) means the current cell spans all rows from the current row to the last row; in reality, however, this feature is not supported in currently available 4.0 browsers.

valign=top|middle|bottom|baseline

Specifies the vertical alignment of the text (or other elements) within the table cell. The default is middle.

width=*number*

Specifies the width of the cell in number of pixels or by a percentage value relative to the table width. The width specified in the first row will apply to the rest of the cells in the column and the values need to be consistent for cells in the column. This attribute has been deprecated in the W3C HTML 4.0 Specification.

Internet Explorer 2.0 and higher only

bordercolor=*#rrggbb* or *color name*

Defines the border color for the cell.

bordercolorlight=#*rrggbb* or *color name*
Defines the dark shadow color for the cell border.

bordercolordark=#*rrggbb* or *color name*
Defines the light highlight color of the cell border.

New in HTML 4.0 Specification
abbr=*text*
Provides an abbreviated form of the cell's content.

axis=*text*
Places a cell into a conceptual category, which could then be used to organize the table in different ways.

headers=*id reference*
Lists header cells (by id) that provide header information for the current data cell. This is intended to make tables more accessible to non-visual browsers.

scope=row|col|rowgroup|colgroup
Specifies groups of data cells for which the current header cell is applicable. This is intended to make tables more accessible to non-visual browsers.

\<textarea\>   \<textarea\>...\</textarea\>

NN: 2, 3, 4 · MSIE: 2, 3, 4, 5 · HTML 4 · WebTV · Opera3

Used within a \<form\>, defines a multiline text-entry form element. The text that is enclosed within the \<textarea\> tags will be displayed in the text-entry field when the form initially displays.

cols=*number*
Specifies the visible width of the text-entry field, measured in number of characters (required). Users may enter text lines that are longer than the provided width, in which case the entry will scroll to the right (or wrap if the browser provides some mechanism for doing so).

---

name=*text*
> Specifies a name for the parameter to be passed to the form-processing application (required).

rows=*number*
> Specifies the height of the text-entry field in numbers of lines of text (required). If the user enters more lines than are visible, the text field scrolls down to accommodate the extra lines.

wrap=off|virtual|physical|soft|hard
> *Internet Explorer 4.0 and Navigator 2.0 and higher only.* Sets word wrapping within the text area.

> off turns word wrapping off; users must enter their own line returns.

> virtual displays the wrap, but the line endings are not transmitted to the server.

> physical displays and transmits line endings to the server.

> soft is the same as virtual.

> hard is the same as physical.

\<tfoot\>   \<tfoot\>...\</tfoot\>

NN: 2, 3, 4 · **MSIE: 2, 3, 4, 5** · **HTML 4** · WebTV · Opera3

Used within a \<table\>, defines the foot of a table and should contain information about a table's columns. It is one of the "row group" tags introduced by Internet Explorer and proposed in the W3C HTML 4.0 Specification (see \<tbody\>) and must contain at least one row (\<tr\>). Its end tag is optional.

Attributes

align=left|center|right|justify|char
> Specifies horizontal alignment (or justification) of cell contents.

---

char=*character*

> Specifies an alignment character; the cell contents will be aligned along this character. The default character is a decimal point (language-appropriate).

charoff=*length*

> Specifies the distance to the first alignment character (char) on each line. If a line doesn't use an alignment character, it should be horizontally shifted to end at the alignment position.

valign=top|middle|bottom|baseline

> Specifies vertical alignment of cell contents.

<th>   <th>...</th>

NN: 2, 3, 4 · MSIE: 2, 3, 4, 5 · HTML 4 · WebTV · Opera3

Used within a <table>, defines a table header cell. Table header cells function the same as table data cells (<td>). Browsers generally display the content of table header cells in bold text centered horizontally and vertically in the cell (although some browsers vary). The end tag is optional.

Attributes

> The <th> tag uses the same attributes as the <td> tag. See listing under <td>.

<thead>   <thead>...</thead>

NN: 2, 3, 4 · MSIE: 2, 3, 4, 5 · HTML 4 · WebTV · Opera3

Used within a <table>, defines the head of the table and should contain information about a table. It must contain at least one row (<tr>). <thead> is one of the "row group" tags introduced by Internet Explorer and proposed in the W3C HTML 4.0 Specification (see <tbody>). Its end tag is optional.

Attributes

align=left|center|right|justify|char

 Specifies horizontal alignment (or justification) of cell contents.

char=*character*

 Specifies a character along which the cell contents will be aligned. The default character is a decimal point (language-appropriate).

charoff=*length*

 Specifies the distance to the first alignment character (char) on each line. If a line doesn't use an alignment character, it should be horizontally shifted to end at the alignment position.

valign=top|middle|bottom|baseline

 Specifies vertical alignment of cell contents.

<title>   <title>...</title>

NN: 2, 3, 4 · MSIE: 2, 3, 4, 5 · HTML 4 · WebTV · Opera3

Specifies the title of the document. The title generally appears in the top bar of the browser window.

<tr>   <tr>...</tr>

NN: 2, 3, 4 · MSIE: 2, 3, 4, 5 · HTML 4 · WebTV · Opera3

Used within a <table>, defines a row of cells within a table. A table row as delimited by <tr> tags contains no content other than a collection of table cells (<td>). The end tag is optional.

Attributes

align=left|center|right

 Aligns the text (or other elements) within the cells of the current row. This attribute has been deprecated by the

---

W3C HTML 4.0 Spec in favor of positioning with style sheets.

bgcolor=#*rrggbb* or *color name*
> Specifies a color to be used in the row. A row's background color overrides the color specified at the table level.

valign=top|middle|bottom|baseline
> Specifies the vertical alignment of the text (or other elements) within cells of the current row.

Internet Explorer 2.0 and higher only

background=*url*
> Specifies the URL of a graphic to be used as a tile within the row.

bordercolor=#*rrggbb* or *color name*
> Defines the border color for the row.

bordercolorlight=#*rrggbb* or *color name*
> Defines the dark shadow color for the row border.

bordercolordark=#*rrggbb* or *color name*
> Defines the light highlight color of the row border.

\<tt>   <tt>...</tt>

NN: 2, 3, 4 · MSIE: 2, 3, 4, 5 · HTML 4 · WebTV · Opera3

Formats enclosed text as typewriter text. The text enclosed in the <tt> tag will be displayed in a monospaced font such as Courier.

\<u>   <u>...</u>

NN: 2, 3, 4 · MSIE: 2, 3, 4, 5 · HTML 4D · WebTV · Opera3

Enclosed text will be underlined when displayed. It is deprecated in the HTML 4.0 Specification in favor of style sheet controls.

<ul>

<ul> <code><ul>...</ul></code>

NN: 2, 3, 4 · MSIE: 2, 3, 4, 5 · HTML 4 · WebTV · Opera3

Defines the beginning and end of an unordered (bulleted) list, which consists of list items <li>.

Attributes

`compact`

> Displays the list block as small as possible. Not many browsers support this attribute.

`type=disc|circle|square`

> Defines the shape of the bullets used for each list item.

<var> <code><var>...</var></code>

NN: 2, 3, 4 · MSIE: 2, 3, 4, 5 · HTML 4 · WebTV · Opera3

Indicates an instance of a variable or program argument (usually displayed in italic).

<wbr> <code><wbr></code>

NN: 2, 3, 4 · MSIE: 2, 3, 4, 5 · HTML 4 · WebTV · Opera3

Indicates a potential word break point. The <wbr> tag works only when placed within <nobr>-tagged text and causes a line break only if the current line already extends beyond the browser's display window margins.

Tag Groups

The following lists group HTML tags by similar function. See the "Alphabetical HTML Tag List" for complete descriptions of each tag.

Structural Tags

The following tags are used primarily to give the document structure.

```
<base>
<body>
<head>
<html>
<link>
<meta>
<title>
```

Text Tags: Block-level Elements

Block-level elements are always formatted with a line-break before and after, with most adding some amount of additional space above and below as well.

```
<address>
<blockquote>
<dd>
<div>
<dl>
<dt>
<h1> through <h6>
<li>
<ol>
<p>
<ul>
```

Text Tags: Inline Styles

The following tags affect the appearance of text. "Inline" means they can be applied to a string of characters within a block element without introducing line breaks.

```
<b>
<big>
<cite>
<code>
<em>
<font> (deprecated)
```

```
<i>
<kbd>
<pre>
<s> (deprecated)
<samp>
<small>
<span>
<strike> (deprecated)
<strong>
<sub>
<sup>
<tt>
<u> (deprecated)
<var>
```

Text Tags: Logical Styles

Logical or content-based styles describe the enclosed text's meaning, context, or usage and leave rendering of the tag to the browser.

```
<abbr>
<acronym>
<cite>
<code>
<del>
<div>
<em>
<ins>
<kbd>
<q>
<samp>
<span>
<strong>
<var>
```

Text Tags: Physical Styles

Physical styles provide specific display instructions.

```
<b>
<big>
<blink>
```

```
<font>
<i>
<s>
<small>
<strike>
<sub>
<sup>
<tt>
<u>
```

List Tags

```
<dir> (deprecated)
<dl>
<dd>
<dt>
<li>
<menu> (deprecated)
<ol>
<ul>
```

Spacing and Positioning Tags

The following tags give authors control over the line breaks, alignment, and spacing within an HTML document.

```
<br>
<center> (deprecated)
<nobr>
<pre>
<spacer>
<table> (<th>, <tr>, <td>)
<wbr>
```

Linking Tags

The following tags are used to create links from one document to another.

```
<a>
<map> (used in client-side imagemaps)
<area> (used in client-side imagemaps)
```

Table Tags

The following tags are used in the creation and formatting of tables.

```
<caption>
<table>
<td>
<th>
```

The following table tags are supported by HTML 4.0 and Internet Explorer 4.0 and higher.

```
<col>
<colgroup>
<tbody>
<thead>
<tfoot>
```

Frame Tags

Frames are created using the following tags.

```
<frame>
<frameset>
<noframes>
```

Form Tags

The following forms are used to define forms and their elements.

```
<button>
<form>
<input>
    (type=button|checkbox|file|hidden|image|
           password|radio|reset|submit|text)
<option>
<select>
<textarea>
```

The following form tags are supported by HTML 4.0 and Internet Explorer 4.0 and higher.

```
<fieldset>
<label>
<legend>
```

Multimedia Tags

The following tags are used to add multimedia elements to web pages.

```
<applet> (deprecated)
<bgsound>
<embed> (dropped from HTML 4)
<object>
<param>
```

Script Tags

The following tags are used to add scripts to HTML documents.

```
<script>
<noscript>
```

Navigator-only Tags

The following tags are supported only by Navigator.

```
<blink>
<layer>
<keygen>
<multicol>
<nolayer>
<server>
<spacer>
```

Internet Explorer-only Tags

The following tags are supported only by Internet Explorer.

```
<bgsound>
<iframe>
<marquee>
```

HTML 4/Internet Explorer-only Tags

The following tags were introduced in Internet Explorer 4.0 and have been adopted into the W3C HTML 4.0 Specification. As of this printing, no other browsers support these tags.

```
<col>
<colgroup>
<del>
<fieldset>
<ins>
<label>
<legend>
<q>
<tbody>
<tfoot>
<thead>
```

HTML 4-only Tags

The following tags are forward-looking elements introduced in the W3C HTML 4.0 Specification, however, as of this printing, they are not supported by any browsers.

```
<abbr>
<acronym>
<bdo>
<optgroup>
```

Tag Structures

The examples below show the tag structure for common web page elements. When an attribute appears in the tag, it indicates that the attribute is required.

HTML Document

The standard skeletal structure of an HTML document is as follows:

```
<HTML>
  <HEAD>
```

```
      <TITLE>document title</TITLE>
   </HEAD>
   <BODY>
     contents of document
   </BODY>
</HTML>
```

Lists

The following are examples of simple lists.

Definition list

```
<DL>
    <DT>
        <DD>
    <DT>
        <DD>
</DL>
```

Ordered (numbered) list

```
<OL>
    <LI>
    <LI>
    <LI>
</OL>
```

Unordered (bulleted) list

```
<UL>
    <LI>
    <LI>
    <LI>
</UL>
```

Nested lists

```
<OL>
    <LI>
    <LI>
        <UL>
```

```
        <LI>
        <LI>
    </UL>
</OL>
```

Linking Within a Document

The first `<a>` tag specifies a named fragment; the second
`<a>` tag links back to that named fragment.

```
<A NAME="fragmentname">Text</A>
...
<A HREF="#fragmentname">Link to Text</A>
```

Client-side Imagemap

In the example below, the image *graphic.gif* is an
imagemap that contains two clickable areas and uses the
client-side imagemap named *map1*.

```
<MAP NAME="map1">
    <AREA SHAPE="rect" COORDS="123,20,234,40"
    HREF=http://www.oreilly.com/">
    <AREA SHAPE="circ" COORDS="111,50,25"
    HREF="index.html">
</MAP>

<IMG SRC="graphic.gif" USEMAP="map1">
```

Basic Table

The following HTML sample shows the basic structure for a
simple four-cell table. The number of columns is determined by the number of cells (`<td>`) that appear within
each row (`<tr>`). The table in the example below has two
rows and two columns.

```
<TABLE>
    <TR>
        <TD></TD>
        <TD></TD>
    </TR>
```

```
<TR>
    <TD></TD>
    <TD></TD>
</TR>
</TABLE>
```

Framed Document

The following code creates a framed document with two
frames, side by side. The number of columns is established
by the number of measurements listed in the cols attribute.

```
<HTML>
    <HEAD>
        <TITLE>Frame Document</TITLE>
    </HEAD>
    <FRAMESET COLS="*,*">
        <FRAME SRC="doc1.html">
        <FRAME SRC="doc2.html">
    </FRAMESET>
    <NOFRAMES>Your browser does not support
frames.</NOFRAMES>
</HTML>
```

Nested frames

You can place one frameset within another as shown in the
following example.

```
<FRAMESET COLS="*,*">
    <FRAME SRC="doc1.html">
    <FRAMESET ROWS="50,150">
        <FRAME SRC="doc2.html">
        <FRAME SRC="doc3.html">
    </FRAMESET>
</FRAMESET>
```

Character Entity Chart

Characters not found in the normal alphanumeric character
set, such as © or &, must be specified in HTML using character entities. Character entities can be defined by name

---

(&name;) or by numeric value (&#nnn;). The browser inter-
prets the string to display the proper character. Named
entities are preferable because numeric values may be
interpreted differently on different platforms.

Unless otherwise noted, the character entities are part of
the HTML 2.0 and later standards and will work with nearly all available browsers. A "4.0" in the character's
description indicates that character entity is part of the
HTML 4.0 Specification and is supported only by Internet
Explorer and Navigator versions 4.0 and higher. An "N" in
the description indicates that the character is a nonstand-
ard entity.

Number	Name	Symbol	Description
				Horizontal tab

			Line feed

			Carriage return
 			Space
!		!	Exclamation point
"	"	"	Quotation mark
#		#	Hash mark
$		$	Dollar sign
%		%	Percent sign
&	&	&	Ampersand
'		'	Apostrophe
(		(	Left parenthesis
)		)	Right parenthesis
*		*	Asterisk
+		+	Plus sign
,		,	Comma
-		-	Hyphen
.		.	Period
/		/	Slash

Number	Name	Symbol	Description
0-9		0–9	Digits 0–9
:		:	Colon
;		;	Semicolon
<	<	<	Less than
=		=	Equal sign
>	>	>	Greater than
?		?	Question mark
@		@	Commercial at sign
A-Z		A–Z	Letters A–Z
[		[	Left square bracket
\		\	Backslash
]		]	Right square bracket
^		^	Caret
_		_	Underscore
`		`	Grave accent
a-z		a–z	Letters a–z
{		{	Left curly brace
|		|	Vertical bar
}		}	Right curly brace
~		~	Tilde
‚		,	Comma (N)
ƒ		f	Florin (N)
„		”	Right double quote (N)
…		…	Elipsis (N)
†		†	Dagger (N)
‡		‡	Double dagger (N)
ˆ		^	Circumflex (N)
‰		‰	Permil (N)

Number	Name	Symbol	Description
Š		Š	Capital S, caron (N)
‹		'	Left single angle quote (N)
Œ		Œ	Capital OE ligature (N)
‘		'	Left single quote (N)
’		'	Right single quote (N)
“		"	Left double quote (N)
”		"	Right double quote (N)
•		•	Bullet (N)
–		–	En dash (N)
—		—	Em dash (N)
˜		~	Tilde (N)
™		™	Trademark (N)
š		š	Small s, caron (N)
›		'	Right single angle quote (N)
œ		œ	Lowercase oe ligature (N)
Ÿ		Ÿ	Capital Y, umlaut (N)
			Nonbreaking space (4.0)
¡	¡	¡	Inverted exlamation mark (4.0)
¢	¢	¢	Cent sign (4.0)
£	£	£	Pound sign (4.0)
¤	¤	¤	General currency symbol (4.0)
¥	¥	¥	Yen sign (4.0)
¦	¦	¦	Broken vertical bar (4.0)
§	§	§	Section sign (4.0)
¨	¨	¨	Umlaut (4.0)
©	©	©	Copyright (4.0)
ª	ª	ª	Feminine ordinal (4.0)
«	«	«	Left angle quote (4.0)
¬	¬	¬	Not sign (4.0)

Number	Name	Symbol	Description
­	­	–	Soft hyphen (4.0)
®	®	®	Registered trademark (4.0)
¯	¯	¯	Macron accent (4.0)
°	°	°	Degree sign (4.0)
±	±	±	Plus or minus (4.0)
²	²	2	Superscript 2 (4.0)
³	³	3	Superscript 3 (4.0)
´	´	´	Acute accent (4.0)
µ	µ	µ	Micro sign (Greek mu) (4.0)
¶	¶	¶	Paragraph sign (4.0)
·	·	·	Middle dot (4.0)
¸	¸	¸	Cedilla (4.0)
¹	¹	1	Superscript 1 (4.0)
º	º	º	Masculine ordinal (4.0)
»	»	»	Right angle quote (4.0)
¼	¼	1/4	Fraction one-fourth (4.0)
½	½	1/2	Fraction one-half (4.0)
¾	¾	3/4	Fraction three-fourths (4.0)
¿	¿	¿	Inverted question mark (4.0)
À	À	À	Capital A, grave accent
Á	Á	Á	Capital A, acute accent
Â	Â	Â	Capital A, circumflex accent
Ã	Ã	Ã	Capital A, tilde accent
Ä	Ä	Ä	Capital A, umlaut
Å	Å	Å	Capital A, ring
Æ	Æ	Æ	Capital AE ligature
Ç	Ç	Ç	Capital C, cedilla
È	È	È	Capital E, grave accent

Number	Name	Symbol	Description
É	É	É	Capital E, acute accent
Ê	Ê	Ê	Capital E, circumflex accent
Ë	Ë	Ë	Capital E, umlaut
Ì	Ì	Ì	Capital I, grave accent
Í	Í	Í	Capital I, acute accent
Î	Î	Î	Capital I, circumflex accent
Ï	Ï	Ï	Capital I, umlaut
Ð	Ð	Ð	Capital eth, Icelandic
Ñ	Ñ	Ñ	Capital N, tilde
Ò	Ò	Ò	Capital O, grave accent
Ó	Ó	Ó	Capital O, acute accent
Ô	Ô	Ô	Capital O, circumflex accent
Õ	Õ	Õ	Capital O, tilde accent
Ö	Ö	Ö	Capital O, umlaut
×	×	×	Multiply sign (4.0)
Ø	Ø	Ø	Capital O, slash
Ù	Ù	Ù	Capital U, grave accent
Ú	Ú	Ú	Capital U, acute accent
Û	Û	Û	Capital U, circumflex
Ü	Ü	Ü	Capital U, umlaut
Ý	Ý	Ý	Capital Y, acute accent
Þ	Þ	þ	Capital Thorn, Icelandic
ß	ß	ß	Small sz ligature, German
à	à	à	Small a, grave accent
á	á	á	Small a, acute accent
â	â	â	Small a, circumflex accent
ã	ã	ã	Small a, tilde
ä	ä	ä	Small a, umlaut
å	å	å	Small a, ring

Number	Name	Symbol	Description
æ	æ	æ	Small ae ligature
ç	ç	ç	Small c, cedilla
è	è	è	Small e, grave accent
é	é	é	Small e, acute accent
ê	ê	ê	Small e, circumflex accent
ë	ë	ë	Small e, umlaut accent
ì	ì	ì	Small i, grave accent
í	í	í	Small i, acute accent
î	î	î	Small i, circumflex accent
ï	ï	ï	Small i, umlaut
ð	ð	∂	Small eth, icelandic
ñ	ñ	ñ	Small n, tilde
ò	ò	ò	Small o, grave accent
ó	ó	ó	Small o, acute accent
ô	ô	ô	Small o, circumflex accent
õ	õ	õ	Small o, tilde
ö	ö	ö	Small o, umlaut
÷	÷	÷	Division sign (4.0)
ø	ø	ø	Small o, slash
ù	ù	ù	Small u, grave accent
ú	ú	ú	Small u, acute accent
û	û	û	Small u, circumflex accent
ü	ü	ü	Small u, umlaut
ý	ý	ý	Small y, acute accent
þ	þ	þ	Small thorn, Icelandic
ÿ	ÿ	ÿ	Small y, umlaut

Decimal to Hexadecimal
Conversion Chart

dec = hex	dec = hex	dec = hex	dec = hex	dec = hex	dec = hex
0 = 00	43 = 2B	86 = 56	129 = 81	172 = AC	215 = D7
1 = 01	44 = 2C	87 = 57	130 = 82	173 = AD	216 = D8
2 = 02	45 = 2D	88 = 58	131 = 83	174 = AE	217 = D9
3 = 03	46 = 2E	89 = 59	132 = 84	175 = AF	218 = DA
4 = 04	47 = 2F	90 = 5A	133 = 85	176 = B0	219 = DB
5 = 05	48 = 30	91 = 5B	134 = 86	177 = B1	220 = DC
6 = 06	49 = 31	92 = 5C	135 = 87	178 = B2	221 = DD
7 = 07	50 = 32	93 = 5D	136 = 88	179 = B3	222 = DE
8 = 08	51 = 33	94 = 5E	137 = 89	180 = B4	223 = DF
9 = 09	52 = 34	95 = 5F	138 = 8A	181 = B5	224 = E0
10 = 0A	53 = 35	96 = 60	139 = 8B	182 = B6	225 = E1
11 = 0B	54 = 36	97 = 61	140 = 8C	183 = B7	226 = E2
12 = 0C	55 = 37	98 = 62	141 = 8D	184 = B8	227 = E3
13 = 0D	56 = 38	99 = 63	142 = 8E	185 = B9	228 = E4
14 = 0E	57 = 39	100 = 64	143 = 8F	186 = BA	229 = E5
15 = 0F	58 = 3A	101 = 65	144 = 90	187 = BB	230 = E6
16 = 10	59 = 3B	102 = 66	145 = 91	188 = BC	231 = E7
17 = 11	60 = 3C	103 = 67	146 = 92	189 = BD	232 = E8
18 = 12	61 = 3D	104 = 68	147 = 93	190 = BE	233 = E9
19 = 13	62 = 3E	105 = 69	148 = 94	191 = BF	234 = EA
20 = 14	63 = 3F	106 = 6A	149 = 95	192 = C0	235 = EB
21 = 15	64 = 40	107 = 6B	150 = 96	193 = C1	236 = EC
22 = 16	65 = 41	108 = 6C	151 = 97	194 = C2	237 = ED
23 = 17	66 = 42	109 = 6D	152 = 98	195 = C3	238 = EE
24 = 18	67 = 43	110 = 6E	153 = 99	196 = C4	239 = EF
25 = 19	68 = 44	111 = 6F	154 = 9A	197 = C5	240 = F0
26 = 1A	69 = 45	112 = 70	155 = 9B	198 = C6	241 = F1
27 = 1B	70 = 46	113 = 71	156 = 9C	199 = C7	242 = F2
28 = 1C	71 = 47	114 = 72	157 = 9D	200 = C8	243 = F3
29 = 1D	72 = 48	115 = 73	158 = 9E	201 = C9	244 = F4
30 = 1E	73 = 49	116 = 74	159 = 9F	202 = CA	245 = F5
31 = 1F	74 = 4A	117 = 75	160 = A0	203 = CB	246 = F6
32 = 20	75 = 4B	118 = 76	161 = A1	204 = CC	247 = F7
33 = 21	76 = 4C	119 = 77	162 = A2	205 = CD	248 = F8
34 = 22	77 = 4D	120 = 78	163 = A3	206 = CE	249 = F9
35 = 23	78 = 4E	121 = 79	164 = A4	207 = CF	250 = FA
36 = 24	79 = 4F	122 = 7A	165 = A5	208 = D0	251 = FB
37 = 25	80 = 50	123 = 7B	166 = A6	209 = D1	252 = FC
38 = 26	81 = 51	124 = 7C	167 = A7	210 = D2	253 = FD
39 = 27	82 = 52	125 = 7D	168 = A8	211 = D3	254 = FE
40 = 28	83 = 53	126 = 7E	169 = A9	212 = D4	255 = FF
41 = 29	84 = 54	127 = 7F	170 = AA	213 = D5	
42 = 2A	85 = 55	128 = 80	171 = AB	214 = D6	

Color Names

Colors can be identified by one of 140 color names originally developed for the X Window System. The complete list appears below.

Color names are only supported by Navigator versions 2.0 and higher and Internet Explorer versions 3.0 and higher. Internet Explorer 2.0 supports the following 16 color names:

aqua	gray	navy	silver
black	green	olive	teal
blue	lime	purple	white
fuschia	maroon	red	yellow

Of the 140 color names, only 10 represent nondithering colors from the Web Palette. They are: aqua, black, blue, cyan, fuschia, lime, magenta, red, white, and yellow.

When viewed on an 8-bit display, the remaining 130 colors will shift to their nearest Web Palette equivalent (or System Palette color). In many cases, the difference is drastic. Many of the pastels shift to solid white.

The "Nearest Web-safe Color" column lists the color that will actually be displayed for each color name on an 8-bit display.

Color Name	RGB Values	Hexa-decimal	Nearest Web-safe Color
aliceblue	240 - 248 - 255	F0F8FF	FFFFFF
antiquewhite	250 - 235 - 215	FAEBD7	FFFFCC
aqua	0 - 255 - 255	00FFFF	00FFFF
aquamarine	127 - 255 - 212	7FFFD4	66FFCC
azure	240 - 255 - 255	F0FFFF	FFFFFF
beige	245 - 245 - 220	F5F5DC	FFFFCC
bisque	255 - 228 - 196	FFE4C4	FFFFCC
black	0 - 0 - 0	000000	000000

Color Name	RGB Values	Hexa-decimal	Nearest Web-safe Color
blanchedalmond	255 - 255 - 205	FFEBCD	FFFFCC
blue	0 - 0 - 255	0000FF	0000FF
blueviolet	138 - 43 - 226	8A2BE2	9933FF
brown	165 - 42 - 42	A52A2A	993333
burlywood	222 - 184 - 135	DEB887	CCCC99
cadetblue	95 - 158 - 160	5F9EA0	669999
chartreuse	127 - 255 - 0	7FFF00	66FF00
chocolate	210 - 105 - 30	D2691E	996600
coral	255 - 127 - 80	FF7F50	FF6666
cornflowerblue	100 - 149 - 237	6495ED	6699FF
cornsilk	255 - 248 - 220	FFF8DC	FFFFCC
crimson	220 - 20 - 60	DC143C	CC0033
cyan	0 - 255 - 255	00FFFF	00FFFF
darkblue	0 - 0 - 139	00008B	000099 [1]
darkcyan	0 - 139 - 139	008B8B	009999
darkgoldenrod	184 - 134 - 11	B8860B	CC9900
darkgray	169 - 169 - 169	A9A9A9	999999 [1]
darkgreen	0 - 100 - 0	006400	006600
darkkhaki	189 - 183 - 107	BDB76B	CCCC66
darkmagenta	139 - 0 - 139	8B008B	990099
darkolivegreen	85 - 107 - 47	556B2F	666633
darkorange	255 - 140 - 0	FF8C00	FF9900
darkorchid	153 - 50 - 204	9932CC	9933CC
darkred	139 - 0 - 0	8B0000	990000 [1]
darksalmon	233 - 150 - 122	E9967A	FF9966
darkseagreen	143 - 188 - 143	8FBC8F	99CC99
darkslateblue	72 - 61 - 139	483D8B	333399
darkslategray	47 - 79 - 79	2F4F4F	333399 [1]
darkturquoise	0 - 206 - 209	00CED1	00CCCC

Color Name	RGB Values	Hexa-decimal	Nearest Web-safe Color
darkviolet	148 - 0 - 211	9400D3	9900CC
deeppink	255 - 20 - 147	FF1493	FF0099
deepskyblue	0 - 191 - 255	00BFFF	00CCFF
dimgray	105 - 105 - 105	696969	666666
dodgerblue	30 - 144 - 255	1E90FF	0099FF
firebrick	178 - 34 - 34	B22222	CC3333
floralwhite	255 - 250 - 240	FFFAF0	FFFFFF
forestgreen	34 - 139 - 34	228B22	339933
fuchsia	255 - 0 - 255	FF00FF	FF00FF
gainsboro	220 - 220 - 220	DCDCDC	CCCCCC [1]
ghostwhite	248 - 248 - 255	F8F8FF	FFFFFF
gold	255 - 215 - 0	FFD700	FFCC00
goldenrod	218 - 165 - 32	DAA520	CC9933
gray	128 - 128 - 128	BEBEBE	999999 [1]
green	0 - 128 - 0	008000	009900
greenyellow	173 - 255 - 47	ADFF2F	99FF33
honeydew	240 - 255 - 240	F0FFF0	FFFFFF
hotpink	255 - 105 - 180	FF69B4	FF66CC
indianred	205 - 92 - 92	CD5C5C	CC6666
indigo	75 - 0 - 130	4B0082	330099
ivory	255 - 240 - 240	FFFFF0	FFFFFF
khaki	240 - 230 - 140	F0D58C	FFCC99
lavender	230 - 230 - 250	E6E6FA	FFFFFF [1]
lavenderblush	255 - 240 - 245	FFF0F5	FFFFFF
lawngreen	124 - 252 - 0	7CFC00	00FF00
lemonchiffon	255 - 250 - 205	FFFACD	FFFFCC
lightblue	173 - 216 - 230	ADD8E6	99CCFF
lightcoral	240 - 128 - 128	F08080	FF9999
lightcyan	224 - 255 - 255	E0FFFF	FFFFFF

Color Name	RGB Values	Hexa-decimal	Nearest Web-safe Color
lightgoldenrodyellow	250 - 250 - 210	FAFAD2	FFFFCC
lightgreen	144 - 238 - 144	90EE90	99FF99
lightgrey	211 - 211 - 211	D3D3D3	CCCCCC[1]
lightpink	255 - 182 - 193	FFB6C1	FFFFCC
lightsalmon	255 - 160 - 122	FFA07A	FF9966
lightseagreen	32 - 178 - 170	20B2AA	33CC99
lightskyblue	135 - 206 - 250	87CEFA	99CCFF
lightslategray	119 - 136 - 153	778899	669999
lightsteelblue	176 - 196 - 222	B0C4DE	CCCCCC
lightyellow	255 - 255 - 224	FFFFE0	FFFFFF
lime	0 - 255 - 0	00FF00	00FF00
limegreen	50 - 205 - 50	32CD32	33CC33
linen	250 - 240 - 230	FAF0E6	FFFFFF
magenta	255 - 0 - 255	FF00FF	FF00FF
maroon	128 - 0 - 0	800000	990000[1]
mediumaquamarine	102 - 205 - 170	66CDAA	66CC99
mediumblue	0 - 0 - 205	0000CD	0000CC
mediumorchid	186 - 85 - 211	BA55D3	CC66CC
mediumpurple	147 - 112 - 219	9370DB	9966CC
mediumseagreen	60 - 179 - 113	3CB371	33CC66
mediumslateblue	123 - 104 - 238	7B68EE	6666FF
mediumspringgreen	0 - 250 - 154	00FA9A	00FF99
mediumturquoise	72 - 209 - 204	48D1CC	33CCCC
mediumvioletred	199 - 21 - 133	C71585	CC0066
midnightblue	25 - 25 - 112	191970	000066[1]
mintcream	245 - 255 - 250	F5FFFA	FFFFFF
mistyrose	255 - 228 - 225	FFE4E1	FFFFFF[1]
moccasin	255 - 228 - 181	FFE4B5	FFFFCC
navajowhite	255 - 222 - 173	FFDEAD	FFCC99

Color Name	RGB Values	Hexa-decimal	Nearest Web-safe Color
navy	0 - 0 - 128	000080	009999[1]
oldlace	253 - 245 - 230	FDF5E6	FFFFFF
olive	128 - 128 - 0	808000	999900
olivedrab	107 - 142 - 35	6B8E23	669933
orange	255 - 165 - 0	FFA500	FF9900
orangered	255 - 69 - 0	FF4500	FF3300
orchid	218 - 112 - 214	DA70D6	CC66CC
palegoldenrod	238 - 232 - 170	EEE8AA	FFFF99
palegreen	152 - 251 - 152	98FB98	99FF99
paleturquoise	175 - 238 - 238	AFEEEE	99FFFF
palevioletred	219 - 112 - 147	DB7093	CC6699
papayawhip	255 - 239 - 213	FFEFD5	FFFFCC
peachpuff	255 - 218 - 185	FFDAB9	FFCCCC
peru	205 - 133 - 63	CD853F	CC9933
pink	255 - 192 - 203	FFC0CB	FFCCCC
plum	221 - 160 - 221	DDA0DD	CC99CC
powderblue	176 - 224 - 230	B0E0E6	CCFFFF
purple	128 - 0 - 128	800080	990099
red	255 - 0 - 0	FF0000	FF0000
rosybrown	188 - 143 - 143	BC8F8F	CC9999
royalblue	65 - 105 - 225	4169E1	3366FF
saddlebrown	139 - 69 - 19	8B4513	993300
salmon	250 - 128 - 114	FA8072	FF9966
sandybrown	244 - 164 - 96	F4A460	FF9966
seagreen	46 - 139 - 87	2E8B57	339966
seashell	255 - 245 - 238	FFF5EE	FFFFFF
sienna	160 - 82 - 45	A0522D	996633
silver	192 - 192 - 192	C0C0C0	CCCCCC
skyblue	135 - 206 - 235	87CEEB	99CCFF

Color Name	RGB Values	Hexa-decimal	Nearest Web-safe Color
slateblue	106 - 90 - 205	6A5ACD	6666CC
slategray	112 - 128 - 144	708090	669999
snow	255 - 250 - 250	FFFAFA	FFFFFF
springgreen	0 - 255 - 127	00FF7F	00FF66
steelblue	70 - 130 - 180	4682B4	3399CC
tan	210 - 180 - 140	D2B48C	CCCC99
teal	0 - 128 - 128	008080	009999
thistle	216 - 191 - 216	D8BFD8	CCCCCC[1]
tomato	253 - 99 - 71	FF6347	FF6633
turquoise	64 - 224 - 208	40E0D0	33FFCC
violet	238 - 130 - 238	EE82EE	FF99FF
wheat	245 - 222 - 179	F5DEB3	FFCCCC
white	255 - 255 - 255	FFFFFF	FFFFFF
whitesmoke	245 - 245 - 245	F5F5F5	FFFFFF
yellow	255 - 255 - 0	FFFF00	FFFF00
yellowgreen	154 - 205 - 50	9ACD32	66CC33

[1] These color names shift to the nearest Mac system palette color when viewed on a Macintosh using any browser except Navigator 4.0 (which shifts it to the nearest Web Palette color).